Christopher Badger is a barrister at 6 Pump Court where he specialises in environmental enforcement, acting for both corporate and individual defendants and on behalf of the Environment Agency. He edits '*Environmental Law News*', and has contributed to previous environmental law books. He has twice has been asked to speak at the Environment Agency's National Conference and was appointed to the 'A' List of Specialist Regulatory Counsel in June 2012.

Chris is ranked as the 'Star Individual' in environmental law in the Chambers & Partners UK Bar Guide.

Stuart Jessop is a specialist regulatory and public law barrister practising from 6 Pump Court, Temple, London. He is ranked in the legal 500 directory as a leading junior in Environmental law and is on the 'A' panel of specialist advocates for the Environment Agency. He has a particular interest in the law in respect of waste, water and nuisance but his practice extends to all aspects of environmental law. He has a wealth of experience advising on enforcement powers of regulators and in judicial review of regulator's decisions.

A Practical Guide to Environmental Enforcement

A Practical Guide to Environmental Enforcement

Christopher Badger
Barrister, Six Pump Court, London

Stuart Jessop
Barrister, Six Pump Court, London

Law Brief Publishing

Published 2021 by Law Brief Publishing, an imprint of Law Brief Publishing Ltd
30 The Parks
Minehead
Somerset
TA24 8BT

www.lawbriefpublishing.com

Paperback: 978-1-912687-09-1

CONTENTS

CHAPTER ONE
INTRODUCTION TO ENVIRONMENTAL ENFORCEMENT

The law on environmental enforcement may be considered as a little niche. It can be incredibly complex, drawing on law from the domestic sphere as well as the European Union. For the large part, public policy dictates that may of the offences should considered as strict liability, which itself raises interesting questions over decisions to prosecute and the most appropriate ways of dealing with particular environmental incidents.

There is a veritable toolbox of potential enforcement responses, ranging from enforcement and suspension notices, to prosecutions, to resolution of cases by way of a civil penalty, often in the form of an enforcement undertaking incorporating a charitable donation to a body benefiting the environment. Furthermore, the introduction of the Definitive Guideline for sentencing environmental offences has seen a significant increase in the level of penalties being imposed for environmental offences. Penalties, almost always linked to turnover, can now be measured in the hundreds of thousands, even millions.

It is against this background that we have sought to provide a practical guide to environmental enforcement. Unfortunately, in a book of this size, it simply isn't possible to provide a fully comprehensive guide to the topic. But we hope that the detail in the book will prove to be a useful practical guide to the main topics in the field of environmental enforcement and the likely issues that arise and how they have been considered by the Courts.

As ever, environmental law will not remain static. It is an ever-developing field. The legislation referred to is current as of 3 November 2020. Legislation necessarily refers to the English versions. There may be differences for Wales and Scotland, although the relevant cases cited may be of assistance.

CHAPTER TWO CORPORATE CRIMINAL LIABILITY

Corporations and Organisations

There are competing principles of attribution of criminal liability, which are themselves not exclusive of each other, namely the 'identification doctrine' (following the principles set out in *Meridian Global Funds Management Asia Ltd v Securities Commission*[1]) and the doctrine of vicarious liability. Corporate responsibility is not just limited to those cases where the individuals responsible for the criminal acts are of such sufficient seniority within the organisation such that they act as the controlling mind of the company.

In the context of criminal law, it is possible to identify yet another broad extension of the principle of vicarious liability, when considering types of offences that carry with them a particular social or public interest in ensuring a wide ambit of liability, often justifying a form of strict liability. In the context of environmental criminality, two cases highlight the strict nature of legal liability for corporate wrongdoing. In *National Rivers Authority (Southern Region) v Alfred McAlpine Homes East Ltd*[2] the High Court stated:

> " ... to make the offence an effective weapon in the defence of environmental protection a company must by necessary implication be criminally liable for the acts or omissions of its servants or agents during activities being done for the company. I do not find that this offends our concept of a just and fair criminal legal system having regard to the magnitude of environmental pollution even though no due diligence defence was provided for."

---

[1] [1995] 2 AC 500

[2] [1994] Env LR 198

In *Environment Agency v Empress Car Co. (Abertillery) Ltd*[3] the House of Lords summarised the principles as follows:

> "(1) Justices dealing with prosecutions for "causing" pollution under section 85(1) should first require the prosecution to identify what it says the defendant did to cause the pollution. If the defendant cannot be said to have done anything at all, the prosecution must fail: the defendant may have "knowingly permitted" pollution but cannot have caused it.
>
> The prosecution need not prove that the defendant did something which was the immediate cause of the pollution: maintaining tanks, lagoons or sewage systems full of noxious liquid is doing something, even if the immediate cause of the pollution was lack of maintenance, a natural event or the act of a third party.
>
> When the prosecution has identified something which the defendant did, the justices must decide whether it caused the pollution. They should not be diverted by questions like "What was the cause of the pollution?" or "Did something else cause the pollution?" because to say that something else caused the pollution (like brambles clogging the pumps or vandalism by third parties) is not inconsistent with the defendant having caused it as well.
>
> If the defendant did something which produced a situation in which the polluting matter could escape but a necessary condition of the actual escape which happened was also the act of a third party or a natural event, the justices should consider whether that act or event should be regarded as a normal fact of life or something extraordinary. If it was in the general run of things a matter of ordinary occurrence, it will not negative the causal effect of the defendant's acts, even if it was not foreseeable that it would happen to that particular defendant or take that particular form. If it can be regarded as

[3] [1999] 2 AC 22

something extraordinary, it will be open to the justices to hold that the defendant did not cause the pollution.

The distinction between ordinary and extraordinary is one of fact and degree to which the justices must apply their common sense and knowledge of what happens in the area."

Consequently, corporations can be guilty of criminal activity where their activities have, as a matter of fact, caused pollution, irrespective of whether that cause was not the immediate cause of the pollution and irrespective of whether such pollution was reasonably foreseeable. Factually therefore, the criminal acts of agents or employees acting within the course of their employment will result in criminal liability for the organisation, regardless of whether those persons can be said to be exercising the controlling mind and will of the company.

The caveat to this principle applies where the particular criminal offence in question concerns an element of *mens rea*. In such circumstances, intention can only be attributed to a company where the relevant person can be shown to be part of the controlling mind and will of the company[4].

Unincorporated Associations

It is instructive to compare and contrast the approach of the criminal courts to associations of individuals which are not incorporated. In *R v L and another* [5] the underground pipework of an oil storage tank belonging to a golf club leaked and polluted a watercourse. The club was an unincorporated association consisting of its members. Two of its officers, who lacked any personal culpability, were charged with the strict liability offence of causing polluted matters to enter controlled waters.[6] The Court of Appeal held that an unincorporated association was by operation of the Interpretation Act 1978 a 'person' for the purposes of that offence

[4] See *R v St Regis Paper Co. Ltd* [2011] EWCA Crim 2527; [2012] PTSR 871
[5] [2008] EWCA Crim 1970; [2009] PTSR 119
[6] then an offence under s.85 of the Water Resources Act 1991; see the *Abertillery* case, above

and identified many other statutes in which, in varied forms, the concept of criminal liability of an unincorporated association was either explicit of implicit. The Court emphasised that its observations were limited to strict liability offences, recognising that very different considerations would arise in the case of any offence involving *mens rea*. The Court also emphasised the co-existing criminal liability of all the members of an unincorporated association; in the case under consideration, all 900-odd members of the club could have been prosecuted as equally primarily liable.

In *R v Lear*[7] the two partners in a hotel business were individually prosecuted for health and safety offences following the death of a guest in a fall through a low sash window. Liability was strict[8]. The Court of Appeal applied *R v L* "*a fortiori*"[9] and held that both the partnership and the individual partners could be prosecuted.

The logic is inescapable and remorseless but its consequences are problematical. In *R v L* the Court identified five different types of statutory provision concerning the criminal liability of unincorporated associations: (i) stipulating that the association shall be prosecuted in its own name and that the members shall not be prosecuted; (ii) limiting the criminal liability of members to cases where they have personal culpability ("officers' liability clauses"); (iii) making any fine payable from the funds of the association, as distinct from those of any member personally; (iv) providing for the rules of service applicable to corporations to be adapted to unincorporated associations; and (v) applying procedural provisions primarily directed to corporate defendants. These serve to identify the nature of the problems. Statutes creating strict liability offences might contain all, some or none of these provisions.

Difficult questions can arise as to how a sentencing court is to approach the question of the defendant(s)' means. Whilst in the case of a business partnership, particularly one comprising only a few partners, it might well seem right to look beyond the assets of the partnership to those of the individual partners, that is not obviously so in the case of the

---

[7] [2018] EWCA Crim 69; [2018] 2 Cr App R 11
[8] Subject to a 'reasonable practicability' defence
[9] *per* Sir Brian Leveson at [41]

members of a golf club. *R v W Stevenson & Sons*[10] concerned strict liability offences under the Sea Fishing (Enforcement of Community Control Measures) Order 2000, which contained an officers' liability provision specifically applicable to partnerships. The Court of Appeal held that the terms of this provision made it clear that a partnership could be prosecuted in its name and that individual partners could only be prosecuted if possessed of the *mens rea* stipulated in the officers' liability provision. The Court further held (with reasoning of more general application) that if the partnership was prosecuted and convicted, any fine imposed could only be levied against the assets of the partnership and the individual partners would not then be 'offenders' for the purpose of confiscation proceedings.

[10] [2008] EWCA Crim 273; [2008] Bus LR 1200

CHAPTER THREE
INDIVIDUAL LIABILITY

Introduction

An individual may commit an offence as a principal. Environmental offending is not limited to corporates.

There are also a number of ways in which a director or other officer of the company may find themselves jointly liable with the company itself. Liability can occur in a number of ways, for example as a principal, by way of joint enterprise, as part of a form of direct liability (for example in the context of fraudulent trading) or most commonly, by way of parasitic liability through consent, connivance or neglect[11]. These particular terms are generally found within the terms of the relevant statute or statutory instrument that creates the particular criminal liability[12].

Reg 41 Environmental Permitting (England and Wales) Regulations 2016

41.— Offences by bodies corporate

(1) If an offence committed under these Regulations by a body corporate is proved—

(a) to have been committed with the consent or connivance of an officer, or

(b) to be attributable to any neglect on the part of an officer,

---

[11] Where there is such an 'officers' liability clause', it does not create a freestanding offence; the offence of which the officer is guilty is that of the company – *R v Wilson* [2013] EWCA Crim 1780; [2014] QB 704

[12] e.g. regulation 41(1) of the Environmental Permitting (England & Wales) Regulations 2016

> the officer as well as the body corporate is guilty of the offence and liable to be proceeded against and punished accordingly.
>
> (2) If the affairs of a body corporate are managed by its members, paragraph (1) applies in relation to the acts and defaults of a member in connection with the member's functions of management as if the member were a director of the body.
>
> (3) In paragraph (1), *"officer"*, in relation to a body corporate, means a director, member of the committee of management, chief executive, manager, secretary or other similar officer of the body, or a person purporting to act in any such capacity.

General observations

The circumstances will vary from case to case. In some cases, as where the officer's place of activity was remote from the workplace or what was done was not under his immediate direction or control, then detailed evidence may be required before a finding of neglect may be legitimately made. The parasitic liability is primarily concerned to provide a penal sanction against those persons charged with functions of management who can be shown to have been responsible for the commission of an offence by a body corporate, and the functions of the office held will be a highly relevant consideration.

Consent

Huckerby v Elliot[13]:

> "It would seem that where a director consents to the commission of an offence by his company, he is well aware of what is going on and agrees to it".

[13] [1970] 1 All E.R. 189

Connivance

'Connivance' implies acquiescence in a course of conduct reasonably likely to lead to the commission of the offence. It necessarily includes knowledge of the criminality, coupled with a failure to prevent that criminality (assuming that the individual concerned had a power to be able to prevent it).

Huckerby v Elliot:

> "Where he *[the director or officer]* connives at the offence committed by the company, he is equally well aware of what is going on but his agreement is tacit, not actively encouraging what happens but letting it continue and saying nothing about it."

Neglect

In the context of a prosecution for breach of s.2 of the Health and Safety at Work Act 1974, the House of Lords in *R v Chargot*[14] stated:

> "Where it is shown that the body corporate failed to achieve or prevent the result that those sections contemplate, it will be a relatively short step for the inference to be drawn that there was connivance or neglect on his part if the circumstances under which the risk arose were under the direction or control of the officer. The more remote his area of responsibility is from those circumstances, the harder it will be to draw that inference."

Re: City Equitable Fire Insurance Co. [1925] Ch. 407

> "(1.) A director need not exhibit in the performance of his duties a greater degree of skill than may reasonably be expected from a person of his knowledge and experience. A

[14] [2008] UKHL 73; [2009] 1 W.L.R. 1

director of a life insurance company, for instance, does not guarantee that he has the skill of an actuary or of a physician. In the words of Lindley M.R.: "If directors act within their powers, if they act with such care as is reasonably to be expected from them, having regard to their knowledge and experience, and if they act honestly for the benefit of the company they represent, they discharge both their equitable as well as their legal duty to the company": see *Lagunas Nitrate Co. v. Lagunas Syndicate.* It is perhaps only another way of stating the same proposition to say that directors are not liable for mere errors of judgment. (2.) A director is not bound to give continuous attention to the affairs of his company. His duties are of an intermittent nature to be performed at periodical board meetings, and at meetings of any committee of the board upon which he happens to be placed. He is not, however, bound to attend all such meetings, though he ought to attend whenever, in the circumstances, he is reasonably able to do so. (3.) In respect of all duties that, having regard to the exigencies of business, and the articles of association, may properly be left to some other official, a director is, in the absence of grounds for suspicion, justified in trusting that official to perform such duties honestly."

Re Hughes [1943] Ch 296

'Neglect' implies a "failure to perform a duty of which the person knows or ought to know".

<u>Director, member of the committee of management, chief executive, manager, secretary or other similar officer of the body, or a person purporting to act in any such capacity, or a person purporting to act in any such capacity</u>

Armour v Skeen [1977] I.R.L.R. 310

"It was said, however, that the appellant did not fall within the class of "manager", secretary or other similar officer of the body corporate, or a person who was purporting to act in any such capacity." Reference was made to *Tesco (Supermarkets) Ltd. v. Natrass [1972] A.C. 153*. It was held in that case that the manager of one of many stores within a large organisation was not a "manager" within a similar provision to section 37 (1) in (section 20 of) the Trade Descriptions Act 1968 (cap. 29). Each case will depend on its particular facts, and on this issue will turn on the actual part played in the organisation."

R v Boal [1992] 3 All E.R. 177

"The intended scope of section 23 [of the Fire Precautions Act 1971] is, we accept, to fix with criminal liability only those who are in a position of real authority, the decision-makers within the company who have both the power and responsibility to decide corporate policy and strategy. It is to catch those responsible for putting proper procedures in place; it is not meant to strike at underlings."

Woodhouse v Walsall MBC [1994] Env L.R. 30

"Merely to speak of "in real authority" amounts, in my judgment, to nothing. They did not finish Simon Brown L.J.'s sentence. Had they done so it seems to me that they could not possibly have arrived at the conclusion that they did, because there was nothing in the evidence which could properly have led them to conclude that the appellant was a decision-maker within the company having both the power and responsibility to decide corporate policy and strategy."

S.157 Environmental Protection Act 1990

157.— Offences by bodies corporate.

(1) Where an offence under any provision of this Act committed by a body corporate is proved to have been committed with the consent or connivance of, or to have been attributable to

> any neglect on the part of, any director, manager, secretary or other similar officer of the body corporate or a person who was purporting to act in any such capacity, he as well as the body corporate shall be guilty of that offence and shall be liable to be proceeded against and punished accordingly.
>
> (2) Where the affairs of a body corporate are managed by its members, subsection (1) above shall apply in relation to the acts or defaults of a member in connection with his functions of management as if he were a director of the body corporate.

In force: 1 January 1991

General observations

There is little difference in substance between s.157 and Reg 41. One observation to be made is that all 3 means of committing the offence are all wrapped up within s.157(1), rather than being split as it appears in Reg 41 between Reg 41(1)(a) and Reg 41(1)(b). This actually makes it a little easier to draft the appropriate charge or indictment when using s.157.

S.158 Environmental Protection Act 1990

> **158. Offences under Parts I, II, IV, VI, etc. due to fault of others.**
>
> Where the commission by any person of an offence under Part I , II , IV , or VI , or section 140 , 141 or 142 above is due to the act or default of some other person, that other person may be charged with and convicted of the offence by virtue of this section whether or not proceedings for the offence are taken against the first-mentioned person.

In force: 1 April 1991

General observations

This section can be used to charge and convict persons whose acts or defaults result in the commission of a criminal offence by other legal persons. For example, this could be used to prosecute employees whose acts or defaults result in a criminal offence being committed by their employer. Note that the section does not state "is due *in whole or in part*", leaving open arguments on causation.

CHAPTER FOUR
INVESTIGATORY POWERS

Introduction

The Environment Agency is one of the regulators responsible for the enforcement of environmental law and the prosecution of environmental crime in England. Note that other regulators responsible for environmental compliance include local authorities, Natural England, Natural Resources Wales ("NRW") for Wales and the Scottish Environmental Protection Agency ("SEPA") in Scotland.

The functions of the Environment Agency derive from the aims and functions ascribed to it by the Environment Act 1995. Section 4 of the Environment Act 1995 describes the principal aim of the Environment Agency in discharging its functions "so to protect or enhance the environment, taken as a whole, as to make the contribution towards attaining the objective of achieving sustainable development ...". Under section 5, pollution control powers are exercisable for the purpose of "preventing or minimising, or remedying or mitigating the effects of, pollution to the environment.

Against that background, the principal investigatory powers of the Environment Agency are to be found in section 108 of the Environment Act 1995:

S.108 Environment Act 1995

108. - Powers of enforcing authorities and persons authorised by them

(1) A person who appears suitable to an enforcing authority may be authorised in writing by that authority to exercise, in accordance with the terms of the authorisation, any of the powers specified in subsection (4) below for the purpose—

(a) of determining whether any provision of the pollution control enactments or flood risk activity enactments in the case of that authority is being, or has been, complied with;

(b) of exercising or performing one or more of the pollution control functions or flood risk activity functions of that authority; or

(c) of determining whether and, if so, how such a function should be exercised or performed.

(2) A person who appears suitable to the Agency, the Natural Resources Body for Wales or SEPA may be authorised in writing by the Agency, the Natural Resources Body for Wales or, as the case may be, SEPA to exercise, in accordance with the terms of the authorisation, any of the powers specified in subsection (4) below for the purpose of enabling the Agency, the Natural Resources Body for Wales or, as the case may be, SEPA to carry out any assessment or prepare any report which the Agency, the Natural Resources Body for Wales or, as the case may be, SEPA is required to carry out or prepare under section 5(3) or 33(3) above.

(3) Subsection (2) above only applies where the Minister who required the assessment to be carried out, or the report to be prepared, has, whether at the time of making the requirement or at any later time, notified the Agency, the Natural Resources Body for Wales or, as the case may be, SEPA that the assessment or report appears to him to relate to an incident or possible incident involving or having the potential to involve—

(a) serious pollution of the environment,

(b) serious harm to human health, or

(c) danger to life or health.

(4) The powers which a person may be authorised to exercise under subsection (1) or (2) above are—

(a) to enter at any reasonable time (or, in an emergency, at any time and, if need be, by force) any premises which he has reason to believe it is necessary for him to enter;

(b) on entering any premises by virtue of paragraph (a) above, to take with him—

(i) any other person duly authorised by the enforcing authority and, if the authorised person has reasonable cause to apprehend any serious obstruction in the execution of his duty, a constable; and

(ii) any equipment or materials required for any purpose for which the power of entry is being exercised;

(c) to make such examination and investigation as may in any circumstances be necessary;

(d) as regards any premises which he has power to enter, to direct that those premises or any part of them, or anything in them, shall be left undisturbed (whether generally or in particular respects) for so long as is reasonably necessary for the purpose of any examination or investigation under paragraph (c) above;

(e) to take such measurements and photographs and make such recordings as he considers necessary for the purpose of any examination or investigation under paragraph (c) above;

(f) to take samples, or cause samples to be taken, of any articles or substances found in or on any premises which he has power to enter, and of the air, water or land in, on, or in the vicinity of, the premises;

(g) in the case of any article or substance found in or on any premises which the person has power to enter, being an article or substance which appears to that person to have caused or to be likely to cause—

(i) pollution of the environment,

(ii) harm to the environment,

(iii) flooding,

(iv) harm to human health, or

(v) a detrimental impact on drainage,

to cause it to be dismantled or subjected to any process or test (but not so as to damage or destroy it, unless that is necessary);

(h) in the case of any such article or substance as is mentioned in paragraph (g) above, to take possession of it and detain it for so long as is necessary for all or any of the following purposes, namely—

(i) to examine it, or cause it to be examined, and to do, or cause to be done, to it anything which he has power to do under that paragraph;

(ii) to ensure that it is not tampered with before examination of it is completed;

(iii) to ensure that it is available for use as evidence in any proceedings for an offence under the pollution control enactments or flood risk activity enactments in the case of the enforcing authority under whose authorisation he acts or in any other proceedings relating to a variation notice, enforcement notice or prohibition notice under those enactments;

(j) to require any person whom he has reasonable cause to believe to be able to give any information relevant to any examination or investigation under paragraph (c) above to answer (in the absence of persons other than a person nominated by that person to be present and any persons whom the authorised person may allow to be present) such questions as the authorised person thinks fit to ask and to sign a declaration of the truth of his answers;

(k) to require the production of, or where the information is recorded in computerised form, the furnishing of extracts from, any records—

(i) which are required to be kept under the pollution control enactments or flood risk activity enactments for the enforcing authority under whose authorisation he acts, or

(ii) which it is necessary for him to see for the purposes of an examination or investigation under paragraph (c) above,
and to inspect and take copies of, or of any entry in, the records;

(l) to require any person to afford him such facilities and assistance with respect to any matters or things within that person's control or in relation to which that person has responsibilities as are necessary to enable the authorised person to exercise any of the powers conferred on him by this section;

(m) any other power for—

(i) a purpose falling within any paragraph of subsection (1) above, or

(ii) any such purpose as is mentioned in subsection (2) above,
which is conferred by regulations made by the Secretary of State.

(5) The powers which by virtue of subsections (1) and (4) above are conferred in relation to any premises for the purpose of enabling an enforcing authority to determine whether any provision of the pollution control enactments or flood risk activity enactments in the case of that authority is being, or has been, complied with shall include power, in order to obtain the information on which that determination may be made,—

(a) to carry out experimental borings or other works on those premises; and

(b) to install, keep or maintain monitoring and other apparatus there.

(6) Except in an emergency, in any case where it is proposed to enter any premises used for residential purposes, or to take heavy equipment on to any premises which are to be entered, any entry by virtue of this section shall only be effected—
(a) after the expiration of at least seven days' notice of the proposed entry given to a person who appears to the authorised person in question to be in occupation of the premises in question, and

(b) either—

(i) with the consent of a person who is in occupation of those premises; or

(ii) under the authority of a warrant by virtue of Schedule 18 to this Act.

(7) Except in an emergency, where an authorised person proposes to enter any premises and—

(a) entry has been refused and he apprehends on reasonable grounds that the use of force may be necessary to effect entry, or

(b) he apprehends on reasonable grounds that entry is likely to be refused and that the use of force may be necessary to effect entry,

any entry on to those premises by virtue of this section shall only be effected under the authority of a warrant by virtue of Schedule 18 to this Act.

(8) In relation to any premises belonging to or used for the purposes of the United Kingdom Atomic Energy Authority, subsections (1) to (4) above shall have effect subject to section 6(3) of the Atomic Energy Authority Act 1954 (which restricts entry to such premises where they have been declared to be prohibited places for the purposes of the Official Secrets Act 1911).

(9) The Secretary of State may by regulations make provision as to the procedure to be followed in connection with the taking of, and the dealing with, samples under subsection (4)(f) above.

(10) Where an authorised person proposes to exercise the power conferred by subsection (4)(g) above in the case of an article or substance found on any premises, he shall, if so requested by a person who at the time is present on and has responsibilities in relation to those premises, cause anything which is to be done by virtue of that power to be done in the presence of that person.

(11) Before exercising the power conferred by subsection (4)(g) above in the case of any article or substance, an authorised person shall consult—

(a) such persons having duties on the premises where the article or substance is to be dismantled or subjected to the process or test, and

(b) such other persons,

as appear to him appropriate for the purpose of ascertaining what dangers, if any, there may be in doing anything which he proposes to do or cause to be done under the power.

(12) No answer given by a person in pursuance of a requirement imposed under subsection (4)(j) above shall be admissible in evidence in England and Wales against that person in any proceedings, or in Scotland against that person in any criminal proceedings.

(13) Nothing in this section shall be taken to compel the production by any person of a document of which he would on grounds of legal professional privilege be entitled to withhold production on an order for discovery in an action in the High Court or, in relation to Scotland, on an order for the production of documents in an action in the Court of Session.

(14) Schedule 18 to this Act shall have effect with respect to the powers of entry and related powers which are conferred by this section.

(15) In this section—

"authorised person" means a person authorised under subsection (1) or (2) above;

"domestic property" has the meaning given by section 75(5)(a) of the Environmental Protection Act 1990;"

"emergency" means a case in which it appears to the authorised person in question—

(a) that there is an immediate risk of serious harm or that circumstances exist which are likely to endanger life or health, and

(b) that immediate entry to any premises is necessary to verify the existence of that risk or those circumstances or to ascertain the cause of that risk or those circumstances or to effect a remedy,

and for this purpose *"serious harm"* means—

(i) serious pollution of the environment,

(ii) serious harm to the environment,

(iii) serious flooding,

(iv) serious harm to human health, or

(v) a serious detrimental impact on drainage;

"enforcing authority" means —

(a) the Secretary of State;

(b) the Agency;

(bza) the Natural Resources Body for Wales;

(ba) a waste collection authority;

(c) SEPA; or

(d) a local enforcing authority;

"English waste collection authority" has the same meaning as in section 45A of the Environmental Protection Act 1990;

"flood risk activity enactment", in relation to an enforcing authority, means an enactment relating to the flood risk activity functions of that authority;

"flood risk activity functions", in relation to the Agency or the Natural Resources Body for Wales, means the functions

relating to flood risk activities conferred or imposed on it by or under regulations made under section 61 of the Water Act 2014;

"local enforcing authority" means —

(a) a local enforcing authority, within the meaning of Part I of the Environmental Protection Act 1990;

(b) a local authority, within the meaning of Part IIA of that Act, in its capacity as an enforcing authority for the purposes of that Act, in its capacity as an enforcing authority for the purposes of that Part;

(c) a local authority for the purposes of Part IV of this Act or regulations under that Part;

(d) a local authority for the purposes of regulations under section 2 of the Pollution Prevention and Control Act 1999 extending to England and Wales or regulations under section 61 of the Water Act 2014;

"mobile plant" means plant which is designed to move or to be moved whether on roads or otherwise;

"pollution control enactments", in relation to an enforcing authority, means the enactments and instruments relating to the pollution control functions of that authority;

"pollution control functions", in relation to the Agency, the Natural Resources Body for Wales or SEPA, means the functions conferred or imposed on it by or under—

(a) the Alkali, &c, Works Regulation Act 1906;

(b) ...

(c) ...

...

(e) Parts I, IA and II of the Control of Pollution Act 1974;

(f) the Control of Pollution (Amendment) Act 1989;

(g) Parts I, II and IIA of the Environmental Protection Act 1990 (integrated pollution control, waste on land and contaminated land);

(h) Chapter III of Part IV of the Water Industry Act 1991 (special category effluent);

(j) Part III and sections 161 to 161D of the Water Resources Act 1991;

(k) section 19 of the Clean Air Act 1993;

(l) ...

(m) regulations made by virtue of section 2(2) of the European Communities Act 1972, to the extent that the regulations relate to pollution;

(n) in relation to SEPA, regulations under section 2 of the Pollution Prevention and Control Act 1999;

and, in relation to the Agency or the Natural Resources Body for Wales, includes the functions conferred or imposed on, or transferred to, it under section 2 of the Pollution Prevention and Control Act 1999 or regulations under section 61 of the Water Act 2014 but, in relation to the Natural Resources Body for Wales, does not include any functions which were exercisable by the Countryside Council for Wales or the Forestry Commissioners immediately before 1 April 2013 and are functions of that Body by virtue of the Natural Resources Body for Wales (Functions) Order 2013;

"pollution control functions", in relation to a local enforcing authority, means the functions conferred or imposed on, or transferred to, that authority—

(a) by or under Part I or IIA of the Environmental Protection Act 1990;

(b) by or under regulations made by virtue of Part IV of this Act; or

(c) by or under regulations made by virtue of section 2(2) of the European Communities Act 1972, to the extent that the regulations relate to pollution;

and, in relation to an authority in England or Wales, includes the functions conferred or imposed on, or transferred to, that authority under section 2 of the Pollution Prevention and Control Act 1999;

"pollution control functions", in relation to the Secretary of State, means any functions which are conferred or imposed upon him by or under any enactment or instrument and which relate to the control of pollution;

"pollution control functions", in relation to a waste collection authority, means —

(a) in relation to an English waste collection authority, the functions conferred or imposed on it by or under Part 2 of the Environmental Protection Act 1990 (other than sections 45, 45A and 46 of that Act so far as relating to the collection of household waste from domestic property); and

(b) in relation to any other waste collection authority, the functions conferred or imposed on it by or under Part 2 of the Environmental Protection Act 1990;

"premises" includes any land, vehicle, vessel or mobile plant;

"waste collection authority" shall be construed in accordance with section 30(3)(a), (b) and (bb) of the Environmental Protection Act 1990.

(16) Any power to make regulations under this section shall be exercisable by statutory instrument; and a statutory instrument containing any such regulations shall be subject to annulment pursuant to a resolution of either House of Parliament.

In force: 1 September 2018

General Observations

This section provides a comprehensive set of powers of entry and investigation which apply to all enforcing authorities exercising powers of entry and investigation. The enforcing authorities include the Secretary of State, the Environment Agency, the Natural Resources Body for Wales, a waste collection authority, SEPA or a local enforcing authority.

Authorisation to exercise powers

Subsection (1) requires persons to be authorised in writing before being able to exercise powers under s.108(4). Those powers can only be exercisable in respect of the three purposes set out at 108(1).

Assessments and reports

Subsection (2) allows for the authorisation of persons to prepare assessments or reports on behalf of the relevant regulatory bodies.

Powers under subsection (4)

Subsection (4) is really the critical part of s.108, identifying as it does the respective powers of authorised officers.

Entry

An authorised officer may enter at any reasonable time any premises which he has reason to believe it is necessary for him to enter, or, in an emergency, at any time and, if need be, by force. The test of necessity is self-evidently subjective, although it is to be anticipated that there must be reasonable grounds for that belief.

It is unclear whether the test of emergency is subjective or objective. Emergency is defined in subsection (15). However, subsection (1)(c) suggests that the test is subjective.

In the case of residential premises, the power of entry is further restricted by subsection (6) and requires 7 days notice of the proposed entry to be given to the occupier. Even then, entry can only be gained with consent or with a warrant.

Where entry has been refused or is likely to be refused and the use of force may be necessary to effect entry, the power of entry shall only be permitted where a warrant has been issued, in accordance with subsection (7).

Samples

Practitioners should have regard to any published guidance on the taking of samples, in particular whether or not bi-partite or even tri-partite samples should be taken. Similarly, there is specific guidance on the sampling and classification of waste, known as WM3, that has direct application to the issue of whether samples taken are representative and appropriate.

Seizure of evidence

Subsection (4)(i)(iii) permits the retention of any article or substance to ensure that it is available for use as evidence in any proceedings for an offence under the pollution control enactments or flood risk activity enactments or in any other proceedings relating to a variation notice, enforcement notice or prohibition notice.

The power to require answers to questions

Subsection (4)(j) provides the authorised officer with the power to require any person whom he has reasonable cause to believe to be able to give any information relevant to any examination or investigation under paragraph (c) to answer questions and to sign a declaration of truth. Under subparagraph (12), no answer given by a person under this subsection shall be admissible in evidence against that person in any proceedings in England and Wales and in any criminal proceedings in Scotland. This does not prevent the potential admissibility of those answers against other legal persons in criminal proceedings, which could include companies or organisations, subject to the relevant hearsay rules. Failure to comply with an authorised officer's request for information is an offence under section 110(1)(a) of the Environment Act 1995.

Critically, the use of s.108(4)(j) has been restricted by the High Court. In *Walker v Chelmsford City Council* [2020] EWHC 625 (Admin), the Queen's Bench Division held that the power to request information pursuant to section 108(4)(j) of the Environment Act 1995 was not a "free-standing power" but in fact could only be utilised pursuant to the powers of entry found under section 108.

This has important ramifications. S.108(4)(j) cannot be used to write to an individual requiring a response to written questions. It cannot be used unless the request is a face-to-face request for information. It also cannot be used unless the power is being used pursuant to the powers of entry. Consequently, it may well be argued that it is not open to an authorised officer to attempt to use s.108(4)(j) in circumstances where they have not already entered the relevant premises.

This is in marked contrast to the significantly wider interpretation given to section 20 of the Health and Safety at Work etc. Act 1974 found in *R (on the application of Wandsworth LBC) v South Western Magistrates Court* [2003] EWGC 1158 (Admin). The Court in Walker recognised that the wording of the two Acts was essentially identical but saw no difficulty in reaching a conclusion that means that the powers of authorised officers under EA 1995 should be more restrictively interpreted than under the HSWA.

Production of records

The authorised officer can require the production of records required to be kept under the pollution control enactments or flood risk activity enactments or any record which it is necessary to see for the purposes of an examination or investigation under paragraph (c). The officer may inspect or take copies of the records or any entry in the records. There is no direct reference in this subsection to a requirement to the site being inspected to provide facilities for the purposes of photocopying a record, but it may reasonably be implied with reference to subparagraph (4)(l).

Records do not extend to documents subject to legal professional privilege (see subparagraph (13).).

Recent authorities such as *R v Paul Jukes* [2018] 2 Cr.App.R. 9 and *Director of the Serious Fraud Office v Eurasian Natural Resources Corp Ltd* [2019] 1 WLR 791 have created a little uncertainty in the litigation privilege landscape, particularly in the context of regulatory investigations.

The latest relevant authority is *Sports Direct International v. FRC* (CA, 18 February 2020), a case about the powers of regulators to acquire documents from a third party which is not the subject of regulatory notice. It has specific application in the context of the Civil Procedure Rules.

To start with the minor of two points considered by the Court: just because a document has been attached to an email which is privileged, that does not make the document privileged. Legal professional privilege (LPP) does not protect the document or the fact that it was sent to a legal adviser under cover of a privileged communication. The CPR requires the disclosure of all free-standing documents.

Then, as to the second (major) point, the Court of Appeal began by reiterating the common law rule that any regulatory powers intended to override legal professional privilege which have been conferred by Parliament must be very clearly drafted to have that effect. In the absence of express wording, then it is possible for LPP not to apply by reason of a necessary implication of that effect. There is no special rule carving out an exception to the ordinary application of the LPP rule.

Subsection 14: Schedule 18

Schedule 18 includes the grounds for the grant of a s.108 warrant, the requirement on an authorised officer to produce evidence of his designation/authority before exercising s.108 powers, the obligation to leave unattended premises as secure as they were found and the duty to provide compensation in certain circumstances.

Subject to section 108(12) of s.108, information obtained in consequence of the exercise of s.108, with or without the consent of any person, shall be admissible in evidence against that or any other person: Schedule 18, paragraph 4. This has the potential to be extremely wide-ranging and would include the admissibility of hearsay interviews with third parties where such interviews are properly conducted under s.108(4)(j). Section 108(12) prevents answers being given under compulsion pursuant to s.108(4)(j) being admissible against that person.

Application of PACE Code B

Environment Officers are required to "have regard to" Code B of PACE if either the exercise of search and entry depends upon the suspicion that an offence has been committed or where the officer concerned has reasonable grounds for suspecting the commission of an offence, including grounds discovered whilst carrying out a routine inspection[15]. However, in practice, the Environment Agency is highly likely to accept that Code B applies. Pro forma Code B notices are routinely provided by officers to the operators of sites that they suspect to be committing criminal offences.

A notice specifying the purpose of the search, the fact that there is no requirement for consent and explaining that anything seized may be used in evidence must be given to the occupier. A caution must be given to

[15] Section 67(9) PACE 1984

any person reasonably suspected of a criminal offence, including to a person answering questions on behalf of a company.

Failure to comply with Code B can result in evidence being excluded as inadmissible[16]. This applies to all criminal proceedings.

Application of the Protection of Freedoms Act 2012 Code of Practice

Code B does not apply to the exercise of a statutory power to enter premises or to inspect goods, equipment or procedures if the exercise of that power is not dependent on the existence of grounds for suspecting that an offence may have been committed and the person exercising the power has no reasonable grounds for such suspicion.

Such visits are governed by the Protection of Freedoms Act 2012 Code of Practice. The purpose of the Code is to ensure greater consistency in the exercise of powers of entry and greater clarity for those affected by them while upholding effective enforcement.

Failure to follow the Code of Practice can also impact on admissibility of evidence and/or abuse of process applications.

Interviews under caution

Save for s.108(4)(j), the Environment Agency has no power to compel a suspect to be interviewed. Consequently, all PACE interviews are voluntary, meaning that the interviewee is entitled to leave the interview at any time they wish.

In practice, it is unusual if the Environment Agency do not provide a suspect with an opportunity to be interviewed. In fact, from the perspective of the Environment Agency, it could be tactically disadvantageous to not interview a suspect or to attempt to rely on information obtained in writing under compulsion. The former risks that a valuable line of enquiry or possible defence may be missed; the latter risks being unable to admit the evidence in Court due to the manner in which it was obtained.

---

[16] Section 67(11) PACE 1984

It is also common for organisations or individuals to request that interviews are conducted in writing. There can be good reasons for this: environmental incidents may be complex and may require the input of a number of different individuals in order to demonstrate what occurred. It may therefore not be possible for a single individual to provide a helpful account to the Environment Agency orally in a PACE interview situation. Requesting an interview in writing also provides a significant opportunity for legal input and careful consideration of the answers to be provided to the Regulator, which is likely to be in the interests of the interviewee.

Key authorities

R (on the application of Allensway Recycling Ltd) v Environment Agency [2015] EWCA Civ 1289; [2016] 1 W.L.R. 1903; [2016] Env L.R. 16 (CA (Civ Div))

> "A person may be authorised under section 108(1) to exercise, for the stated purposes, any of the powers set out in section 108(4), including the power to enter any premises. Section 108(6), however, limits the circumstances in which the power of entry may be exercised in relation to residential premises. It provides that entry by virtue of section 108 shall only be effected (a) after the expiration of at least seven days' notice to a person who appears to be in occupation of the premises, *and* (b) *either* (i) with the consent of a person who is in occupation of the premises, *or* (ii) under the authority of a warrant by virtue of Schedule 18. The natural meaning of the subsection, having regard to its language and lay-out, including the linking "and" between paragraph (a) and paragraph (b), is clear: in every case there must be at least seven days' notice before entry may be effected, and entry may be effected after the expiry of the notice period only with the consent of an occupier or under the authority of a warrant."

Sweeney v Westminster Magistrates' Court
[2014] EWHC 2068 (Admin); [2014] Env L.R. 27

> "I accept the claimant's submission that the warrant did not identify the offence or offences being investigated with any specificity. It did not identify the nature of the investigation. No real attempt was made to identify with any precision the type and nature of material sought in the search. The business activities of the individuals named on the warrant are neither defined nor limited. The result being that the search could include any material relating to any business activity of any named individual. The fact that a number of companies were identified is diluted by the words "variation or linked to the same". This has to include unidentified companies. The wording does not limit the seizure of material to a fraud investigation nor to documents related to waste dumping or disposal. Given the knowledge possessed, the RART and the EA could have done considerably more to identity the nature of the investigation, limit the parameters of the search to specified business activities of the named individuals and identify the categories of material sought. In my view the warrant did not identify as far as was practicable the articles to be sought in the search in breach of section 15(6)(b) PACE."

Walker v Chelmsford City Council
[2020] EWHC 635 (Admin); [2020] 3 WLUK 619

> "Albeit the observations were *obiter*, I am persuaded by Waller LJ's doubts that section 69(3)(i) applied to anything other than face-to-face requests when relevant premises had been entered. As set out above, section 69(3)(i) was replicated in section 108(4)(j) without alteration, and in my view it can only be assumed that in removing the designation of waste regulation authority from local authorities such as the respondent it was intended that responsibility for making written requests for information would be for the Environment Agency.

25. Notwithstanding the analysis of Scott Baker LJ in *Wandsworth LBC* when dealing with the HSWA, I consider the wording of the subsection 108(4)(j), certainly in the context of this particular legislation, supports the interpretation that it only applies to a face-to-face request for information, for two principal reasons. First, on a plain reading of the subsection, it gives the power to the authorised officer to require a "person" to answer questions with a limited number of other individuals being present, and thereafter to sign a declaration of truth as to his or her answers. I consider it unduly strains the terms of the subsection to suggest that it covers an entirely different scenario, namely posing written questions that are to be answered in writing, a possibility which was not in any sense revealed in the wording of the subsection (in stark contrast to the clear terms of section 71 EPA). Additionally, given the immediately preceding reference to a face-to-face meeting, the requirement of a declaration of truth self-evidently reflects what would be necessary following a verbal exchange, namely a record compiled by the authorised officer, with confirmation as to what had been said evidenced by the signature of the "person"."

S.109 Environment Act 1995

109.— Power to deal with cause of imminent danger of serious pollution etc.

(1) Where, in the case of any article or substance found by him on any premises which he has power to enter, an authorised person has reasonable cause to believe that, in the circumstances in which he finds it, the article or substance is a cause of imminent danger of serious pollution of the environment or serious harm to human health, he may seize it and cause it to be rendered harmless (whether by destruction or otherwise).

(2) As soon as may be after any article or substance has been seized and rendered harmless under this section, the authorised person shall prepare and sign a written report giving particulars of the circumstances in which the article or substance was seized and so dealt with by him, and shall—

(a) give a signed copy of the report to a responsible person at the premises where the article or substance was found by him; and

(b) unless that person is the owner of the article or substance, also serve a signed copy of the report on the owner;

and if, where paragraph (b) above applies, the authorised person cannot after reasonable inquiry ascertain the name or address of the owner, the copy may be served on him by giving it to the person to whom a copy was given under paragraph (a) above.

(3) In this section, *"authorised person"* has the same meaning as in section 108 above.

In force: 1 April 1996

General observations

This section provides a power to seize articles or substances found on premises which there is a power to enter under s.108.

S. 71 Environmental Protection Act 1990

71.— Obtaining of information from persons and authorities.

(2) For the purpose of the discharge of their respective functions under this Part—

(a) the Secretary of State, and

(b) a waste regulation authority,

may, by notice in writing served on him, require any person to furnish such information specified in the notice as the Secretary of State or the authority, as the case may be, reasonably considers he or it needs, in such form and within such period following service of the notice, or at such time, as is so specified.

(2A) A waste collection authority has the power referred to in subsection (2) for the purpose of the discharge of its functions under sections 34B and 34C above.

(3) A person who—

(a) fails, without reasonable excuse, to comply with a requirement imposed under subsection (2) or (2A) above; or
shall be liable—

(i) on summary conviction, to a fine not exceeding the statutory maximum;

(ii) on conviction on indictment, to a fine or to imprisonment for a term not exceeding two years, or to both.

(4) The Secretary of State may, by notice in writing, require a waste regulation authority or waste collection authority in England and Wales to supply to him, or to such other person as may be specified in the notice, such information as may be so specified in respect of–

(a) cases where the authority has exercised any powers under section 59, 59ZA, 59ZB or 59ZC above, and

(b) cases where the authority has taken action under any other enactment in respect of any deposit or other disposal of controlled waste in contravention of section 33(1) above.

In force: 8 May 2018

General Observations

Under this section, the Secretary of State, a waste regulation authority and a waste collection authority can require any person to provide them with such information as specified within the notice as they reasonably consider that they need and within a time period that they specify.

Failure, without a reasonable excuse, to comply with the notice can result in up to 2 years imprisonment.

The protection against self-incrimination

It is not a reasonable excuse to fail to comply with a notice served under s.71 on the ground that the information provided may incriminate the person providing it. Protections against self-incrimination, such as they exist, are to be found in the criminal court's overarching power to exclude evidence under s.78 PACE looking at the prejudice caused, including the circumstances in which the evidence was obtained.

On the topic of self-incrimination, there is a little uncertainty on the extent to which a company can claim a protection against self-incrimination. In *R v Hertfordshire CC ex p. Green Environmental Industries Ltd*[17], the Court of Appeal (not reiterated in the House of Lords) stated that "the right not to give evidence against oneself is basically a right of an individual, not a legal entity or company". In *Walker v Chelmsford CC*[18] the High Court stated that it was "not sure whether that statement necessarily accurately reflects the law of England and Wales" although the Court did not go on to determine the issue either way. It is likely that further consideration needs to be given to this issue by the Courts.

There is also uncertainty over whether an employee can refuse to answer an enquiry on the ground that they may incriminate the company for

[17] [1998] Env. L.R. 153

[18] [2020] EWHC 635 (Admin)

which they work. Again, the topic was touched on in *Walker v Chelmsford CC* but not resolved. The privilege against self-incrimination derives from common law. As a result, it would be open to the Courts to extend the privilege to cover such a scenario if the Courts chose to do so.

Saunders v United Kingdom
[1996] 12 WLUK 363

> "71. The Court does not accept the Government's premise on this point since some of the applicant's answers were in fact of an incriminating nature in the sense that they contained admissions to knowledge of information which tended to incriminate him. In any event, bearing in mind the concept of fairness in Article 6, the right not to incriminate oneself cannot reasonably be confined to statements of admission of wrongdoing or to remarks which are directly incriminating. Testimony obtained under compulsion which appears on its face to be of a non-incriminating nature—such as exculpatory remarks or mere information on questions of fact—may later be deployed in criminal proceedings in support of the prosecution case, for example to contradict or cast doubt upon other statements of the accused or evidence given by him during the trial or to otherwise undermine his credibility. Where the credibility of an accused must be assessed by a jury the use of such testimony may be especially harmful. It follows that what is of the essence in this context is the use to which evidence obtained under compulsion is made in the course of the criminal trial.
>
> ...
>
> 74. Nor does the Court find it necessary, having regard to the above assessment as to the use of the interviews during the trial, to decide whether the right not to incriminate oneself is absolute or whether infringements of it may be justified in particular circumstances.

It does not accept the Government's argument that the complexity of corporate fraud and the vital public interest in the investigation of such fraud and the punishment of those responsible could justify such a marked departure as that which occurred in the present case from one of the basic principles of a fair procedure. Like the Commission, it considers that the general requirements of fairness contained in Article 6, including the right not to incriminate oneself, apply to criminal proceedings in respect of all types of criminal offences without distinction, from the most simple to the most complex. The public interest cannot be invoked to justify the use of answers compulsorily obtained in a non-judicial investigation to incriminate the accused during the trial proceedings. It is noteworthy in this respect that under the relevant legislation statements obtained under compulsory powers by the Serious Fraud Office cannot, as a general rule, be adduced in evidence at the subsequent trial of the person concerned. Moreover the fact that statements were made by the applicant prior to his being charged does not prevent their later use in criminal proceedings from constituting an infringement of the right."

R v Hertfordshire CC ex p. Green Environmental Industries Ltd [2000] 2 A.C. 412; [2000] 2 W.L.R. 373

My Lords, in the process of construction, the public interest in obtaining the information is only one side of the coin. As Lord Mustill said in *R. v. Director of the Serious Fraud Office, ex p. Smith [1993] A.C. 1, 32* , it is necessary also to identify what variety of the right to silence would be affected by the power and the strength of the grounds for preserving it. As I have said, the request under section 71(2) does not in itself form a part, even a preliminary part, of any criminal proceedings. It does not therefore touch the principle which prohibits interrogation of a person charged or accused. Nor is there any question of the potential abuse of investigatory powers which those rules are designed to prevent. The section does not provide for oral interrogation and the recipient of the request may answer upon advice and at his leisure. Nor does the obligation to give the information prejudice the fairness of a possible trial, since the accused would still have the protection of section 78 of the Act of 1984: see Lord Browne-Wilkinson in *Hamilton v. Naviede [1995] 2 A.C. 75, 107.*

Who can a notice be served upon?

A notice may be served on "any person".

Grounds for serving a notice

The information must be such that that the author of the notice "reasonably considers" that he needs it for the purpose of the discharge of the specific functions referred to in the section.

It follows that the request must therefore be made pursuant to the discharge of a specific function. However, in practice this is extremely wide-ranging, particularly in the case of the Environment Agency.

The assessment of necessity is a subjective one.

Reg 61 Environmental Permitting (England and Wales) Regulations 2016

61.— Power to require the provision of information

(1) For the purposes of discharging its functions under these Regulations, an appropriate authority, regulator, exemption registration authority or exemption authority, by notice served on any person, may require that person to provide such information in such form and within such period as is specified in the notice.

(2) A notice under paragraph (1) may require a person to provide any information on emissions where that requirement is reasonable, including the provision of information—

(a) not in the person's possession, and

(b) which would not usually come into the person's possession.

(3) For the purposes of this regulation the discharge by the appropriate authority of—

(a) an obligation of the United Kingdom under the EU Treaties, or

(b) an international obligation of the United Kingdom,
must be treated as a function of the authority under these Regulations.

(4) For the purposes of this regulation the compilation of an inventory of emissions (whether or not from a regulated facility) must be treated as a function of the regulator under these Regulations.

In force: 1 January 2017

<u>For the purpose of discharging its functions under these Regulations</u>

A notice under Regulation 61 may only be served by the Environment Agency for the purpose of discharging its functions under the Environmental Permitting Regulations. Save in the context of emissions, the word "reasonable" does not appear in this Regulation. Failure to comply with such a notice is a criminal offence. As a consequence, organisations and individuals served with such a notice would be best advised to engage with the Regulator in correspondence well in advance of any deadline in the event that the request made appears to be onerous or out of scope of the reason given for the service of the notice in the first place.

S. 116 Environmental Protection Act 1990

116.— Obtaining of information from persons.

(1) For the purposes of the discharge of his functions under this Part, the Secretary of State may, by notice in writing served on any person who appears to him—

(a) to be involved in the importation, acquisition, keeping, release or marketing of genetically modified organisms; or

(b) to be about to become, or to have been, involved in any of those activities;

require that person to furnish such relevant information available to him as is specified in the notice, in such form and within such period following service of the notice as is so specified.

(2) For the purposes of this section *"relevant information"* means information concerning any aspects of the activities in question, including any damage to the environment which may be or have been caused thereby; and the discharge by the Secretary of State of an obligation of the United Kingdom under the EU Treaties or any international agreement concerning the protection of the environment from harm caused by genetically modified organisms shall be treated as a function of his under this Part .

In force: 22 April 2011

This is specifically concerned with genetically modified organisms.

S.111 Environment Act 1995

111.— Evidence in connection with certain pollution offences.

(1) ...

(2) Information provided or obtained pursuant to or by virtue of a condition of a relevant licence (including information so provided or obtained, or recorded, by means of any apparatus) shall be admissible in evidence in any proceedings, whether against the person subject to the condition or any other person.

(2A) Information provided or obtained pursuant to or by virtue of relevant regulations (including information so provided or obtained, or recorded, by means of any apparatus) shall be admissible in evidence in any proceedings, whether against the person subject to a requirement arising under or by virtue of the regulations or any other person.

(3) For the purposes of subsections (2) and (2A) above, apparatus shall be presumed in any proceedings to register or record accurately, unless the contrary is shown or provision otherwise is made by the relevant licence or by virtue of the relevant regulations.

(4) Where—

(a) by virtue of a condition of a relevant licence or by virtue of relevant regulations, an entry is required to be made in any record as to the observance of any condition of the relevant licence or compliance with any requirement arising under or by virtue of the regulations, and

(b) the entry has not been made,
that fact shall be admissible in any proceedings as evidence that that condition has not been observed or that requirement has not been complied with.

(5) In this section—

"apparatus" includes any meter or other device for measuring, assessing, determining, recording or enabling to be recorded,

the volume, temperature, radioactivity, rate, nature, origin, composition or effect of any substance, flow, discharge, emission, deposit or abstraction;

"condition of a relevant licence" includes any requirement to which a person is subject under, by virtue of or in consequence of a relevant licence;

"environmental licence" has the same meaning as it has in Part I above as it applies in relation to the Agency, the Natural Resources Body for Wales or SEPA, as the case may be;

"relevant licence" means —

(a) any environmental licence;

(b) any consent under Part II of the Sewerage (Scotland) Act 1968 to make discharges of trade effluent;

(c) any agreement under section 37 of that Act with respect to, or to any matter connected with, the reception, treatment or disposal of such effluent;

(d) any consent under Chapter III of Part IV of the Water Industry Act 1991 to make discharges of special category effluent; or

(e) any agreement under section 129 of that Act with respect to, or to any matter connected with, the reception or disposal of such effluent.

"relevant regulations" means regulations made for the purpose of implementing the EU ETS Directive (as defined by section 56)

(6) In section 25 of the Environmental Protection Act, after subsection (2) (which makes similar provision to subsection (4) above) there shall be inserted—

> "(3) Subsection (2) above shall not have effect in relation to any entry required to be made in any record by virtue of a condition of a relevant licence, within the meaning of section 111 of the Environment Act 1995 (which makes corresponding provision in relation to such licences)."

In force: 1 April 2015

General observations

Subsection (2)

Information provided or obtained pursuant to or by virtue of a condition of a relevant licence (for which you can also read permit), shall be admissible in evidence in any proceedings.

Operator self-monitoring is an important part of environmental regulation, as it provides sites perceived to be lower risk with the opportunity for less regulatory intervention in exchange to provision to the Environment Agency of information relating to performance and permit compliance. However, it remains the case that this section appears to override any suggestion of protection against self-incrimination where it is a requirement of the permit that information, albeit incriminating, must be supplied to the Regulator.

Subsection (2A)

As above for subsection 2, save that this subsection applies where the information is required as a result of relevant regulations.

Subsection (3)

There is a presumption that the information provided is accurate.

Subsection (4)

Failure to make an entry in a record, where such an entry is required under a licence or permit, is admissible that the condition relating to that particular entry has not been complied with. It would then fall to the operator to demonstrate that the particular condition had been complied with, by reference to other evidence.

Reg 43 Environmental Permitting (England and Wales) Regulations 2016

> **43. Admissibility of evidence**
>
> Where, pursuant to an environmental permit granted by a local authority, an entry is required to be made in any record as to the observance of a condition of the environmental permit and the entry has not been made, that fact is admissible as evidence that the condition has not been observed.

In force: 1 January 2017

This Regulation would appear to be unnecessary, given the existence of section 111 of the Environment Act 1995. It is interesting that the regulation appears to limit the question of admissibility to environmental permits granted by local authorities (defined by Regulation 6), which would exclude the Environment Agency. However, this doesn't appear to have any effect in practice.

CHAPTER FIVE

WASTE OFFENCES

Reg 38 Environmental Permitting (England and Wales) Regulations 2016

38.— Offences

(1) It is an offence for a person to—

(a) contravene regulation 12(1), or

(b) knowingly cause or knowingly permit the contravention of regulation 12(1)(a).

(2) It is an offence for a person to fail to comply with or to contravene an environmental permit condition.

(3) It is an offence for a person to fail to comply with the requirements of an enforcement notice or of a prohibition notice, suspension notice, landfill closure notice, mining waste facility closure notice, flood risk activity emergency works notice or flood risk activity remediation notice.

(4) It is an offence for a person—

(a) to fail to comply with a notice under regulation 61(1) requiring the provision of information, without reasonable excuse;

(b) to make a statement which the person knows to be false or misleading in a material particular, or recklessly to make a statement which is false or misleading in a material particular, where the statement is made—

(i) in purported compliance with a requirement to provide information imposed by or under a provision of these Regulations,

(ii) for the purpose of obtaining the grant of an environmental permit to any person, or the variation, transfer in whole or in part, or surrender in whole or in part of an environmental permit, or

(iii) for the purpose of obtaining, renewing or amending the registration of an exempt facility;

(c) intentionally to make a false entry in a record required to be kept under an environmental permit condition;

(d) with intent to deceive—

(i) to forge or use a document issued or authorised to be issued or required for any purpose under an environmental permit condition, or

(ii) to make or have in the person's possession a document so closely resembling such a document as to be likely to deceive.

(5) It is an offence for an establishment or undertaking to—

(a) fail to comply with paragraph 17(3) or (4) of Schedule 2, or

(b) intentionally make a false entry in a record required to be kept under that paragraph.

(6) If an offence committed by a person under this regulation is due to the act or default of some other person, that other person is also guilty of the offence and liable to be proceeded against and punished accordingly, whether or not proceedings for the offence are taken against the first-mentioned person.

In force: 7 April 2019

Reg 12 Environmental Permitting (England and Wales) Regulations 2016

12.— Requirement for an environmental permit

(1) A person must not, except under and to the extent authorised by an environmental permit—

(a) operate a regulated facility, or

(b) cause or knowingly permit a water discharge activity or groundwater activity.

(1A) Paragraph (1)(a) does not apply in relation to the operation of a medium combustion plant, mobile medium combustion plant or a specified generator comprising—

(a) a new medium combustion plant, before 20th December 2018;

(b) an existing medium combustion plant with a rated thermal input greater than 5 megawatts, before 1st January 2024;

(c) an existing medium combustion plant with a rated thermal input of less than or equal to 5 megawatts, before 1st January 2029;

(d) a specified generator, before the permitting date,
unless that medium combustion plant, mobile medium combustion plant or specified generator, is required to have a permit by virtue of forming part of another class of regulated facility.

(1B) For the purposes of paragraph (1A)—

(a) *"existing medium combustion plant"* and *"new medium combustion plant"* have the meanings given in paragraph 2(1) of Schedule 25A;

(b) *"permitting date"* has the meaning given in paragraph 3(2) of Schedule 25B.

(2) Paragraph (1)(b) does not apply if the water discharge activity or groundwater activity is an exempt facility.

(3) In respect of a radioactive substances activity, paragraph (1) does not apply to a person to whom a radioactive substances exemption applies for that activity.

(4) Paragraph (5) applies to a person ("A") who—

(a) receives radioactive waste from another person ("B") for the purposes of A disposing of that waste, and

(b) subsequently disposes of that waste.

(5) Where this paragraph applies, A does not require an environmental permit—

(a) for the receipt of waste from B, where B holds an environmental permit which allows B to dispose of the waste to A, or

(b) for the subsequent disposal of that waste by A, where the waste is disposed of in accordance with the permit held by B.

Definitions

The terms "waste" and "waste operation" are defined under regulation 2 and "regulated facility", which includes a waste operation, is defined under regulation 8 of the EPR 2016.

In force: 30 January 2018

Reg 40 Environmental Permitting (England and Wales) 2016

40.— Defences

(1) It is a defence for a person charged with an offence under regulation 38(1), (2) or (3) to prove that the acts alleged to constitute the contravention were done in an emergency in order to avoid danger to human health in a case where—

(a) the person took all such steps as were reasonably practicable in the circumstances for minimising pollution, and

(b) particulars of the acts were furnished to the regulator as soon as reasonably practicable after they were done.

(2) A person who knowingly permits a water discharge activity or groundwater activity where the discharge is water from an abandoned mine or an abandoned part of a mine is not guilty of an offence under regulation 38(1) unless—

(a) the person is the owner or former operator of the mine or that part of it, and

(b) the mine or the part of the mine was abandoned after 31st December 1999.

(3) In paragraph (2), *"abandoned"*, in relation to a mine, and *"mine"* have the meaning given in section 91A of the 1991 Act.

In force: 1 January 2017

S.33 Environmental Protection Act 1990

33.— Prohibition on unauthorised or harmful deposit, treatment or disposal etc. of waste.

(1) Subject to subsections (1A), (1B), (2) and (3) below a person shall not—

(a) deposit controlled waste or extractive waste, or knowingly cause or knowingly permit controlled waste or extractive waste to be deposited in or on any land unless an environmental permit authorising the deposit is in force and the deposit is in accordance with the permit;

(b) submit controlled waste, or knowingly cause or knowingly permit controlled waste to be submitted, to any listed operation (other than an operation within subsection (1)(a)) that—

(i) is carried out in or on any land, or by means of any mobile plant, and

(ii) is not carried out under and in accordance with an environmental permit;

(c) treat, keep or dispose of controlled waste or extractive waste in a manner likely to cause pollution of the environment or harm to human health.

(1A) Paragraphs (a) and (b) of subsection (1) above do not apply in relation to a waste operation that is an exempt waste operation.

(1B) Subsection (1) does not apply in relation to any part of a waste operation that—

(a) is the subject of a marine licence under the Marine and Coastal Access Act 2009; or

(b) does not require such a licence by virtue of any provision made by or under section 74, 75 or 77 of that Act and does not involve the dismantling of a ship that is waste.

(2) Subject to subsection (2A) below, paragraphs (a) and (b) of subsection (1) above do not apply in relation to household waste from a domestic property which is treated, kept or disposed of within the curtilage of the property.

(2A) Subsection (2) above does not apply to the treatment, keeping or disposal of household waste by an establishment or undertaking.

(3) Subsection (1)(a), (b) or (c) above do not apply in cases prescribed in regulations made by the Secretary of State and the regulations may make different exceptions for different areas.

(4) The Secretary of State, in exercising his power under subsection (3) above, shall have regard in particular to the expediency of excluding from the prohibitions in subsection (1) —

(a) any deposits which are small enough or of such a temporary nature that they may be so excluded;

(b) any means of treatment or disposal which are innocuous enough to be so excluded;

(c) cases for which adequate controls are provided by another enactment than this section.

(5) Where controlled waste is carried in and deposited from a motor vehicle, the person who controls or is in a position to control the use of the vehicle shall, for the purposes of subsection (1)(a) above, be treated as knowingly causing the waste to be deposited whether or not he gave any instructions for this to be done.

(6) A person who contravenes subsection (1) above commits an offence.

(7) It shall be a defence for a person charged with an offence under this section to prove—

(a) that he took all reasonable precautions and exercised all due diligence to avoid the commission of the offence; or

(b) ...

(c) that the acts alleged to constitute the contravention were done in an emergency in order to avoid danger to human health in a case where—

(i) he took all such steps as were reasonably practicable in the circumstances for minimising pollution of the environment and harm to human health; and

(ii) particulars of the acts were furnished to the waste regulation authority as soon as reasonably practicable after they were done.

(8) Subject to subsection (9) below, a person who commits an offence under this section is liable–

(a) on summary conviction, to imprisonment for a term not exceeding 12 months or a fine or both;

(b) on conviction on indictment, to imprisonment for a term not exceeding five years or a fine or both.
(9) A person (other than an establishment or undertaking) who commits a relevant offence shall be liable on summary conviction, or on conviction on indictment, to a fine.

(10) In this section, *"relevant offence"* means an offence under this section in respect of a contravention of subsection (1)(c) above consisting of the treatment, keeping or disposal within the curtillage of a domestic property of household waste from that property.

(11) For the purposes of subsection (1)(a) above, the deposit of waste in or on land includes any listed operation involving such a deposit.

(12) For the purposes of subsection (1)(c) above, treating, keeping or disposing of controlled waste includes submitting it to any listed operation.

(13) For the purposes of this section, a "listed operation" is an operation listed in Annex I or II of Directive 2008/98/EC of the European Parliament and of the Council of 19 November 2008 on waste.

In force: 20 March 2019

General observations

There are two parallel legislative regimes governing the main waste offences: the Environmental Protection Act 1990 and the Environmental Permitting (England and Wales) Regulations 2016. A significant number of the key concepts within the two regimes are identical, hence these have been dealt with collectively below.

Causing and knowingly permitting

Alphacell Ltd v Woodward[19]

> "The subsection evidently contemplates two things—causing, which must involve some active operation or chain of operations involving as the result the pollution of the stream; knowingly permitting, which involves a failure to prevent the pollution, which failure, however, must be accompanied by knowledge. I see no reason either for reading back the word "knowingly" into the first limb, or for reading the first limb as,

[19] [1972] A.C. 824; [1972] 2 W.L.R. 1320; [1972] 2 All E.R. 475

by deliberate contrast, hitting something which is unaccompanied by knowledge. The first limb involves causing and this is what has to be interpreted.

In my opinion, "causing" here must be given a common sense meaning and I deprecate the introduction of refinements, such as causa causans, effective cause or novus actus. There may be difficulties where acts of third persons or natural forces are concerned but I find the present case comparatively simple. The appellants abstract water, pass it through their works where it becomes polluted, conduct it to a settling tank communicating directly with the stream, into which the polluted water will inevitably overflow if the level rises over the overflow point. They plan, however, to recycle the water by pumping it back from the settling tank into their works: if the pumps work properly this will happen and the level in the tank will remain below the overflow point. It did not happen on the relevant occasion due to some failure in the pumps.

In my opinion, this is a clear case of causing the polluted water to enter the stream. The whole complex operation which might lead to this result was an operation deliberately conducted by the appellants and I fail to see how a defect in one stage of it, even if we must assume that this happened without their negligence, can enable them to say they did not cause the pollution. In my opinion, complication of this case by infusion of the concept of mens rea, and its exceptions, is unnecessary and undesirable. The section is clear, its application plain. I agree with the majority of the Divisional Court, who upheld the conviction, except that rather than say that the actions of the appellants were a cause of the pollution I think it more accurate to say that the appellants caused the polluting matter to enter the stream."

Environment Agency v Empress Car Co. (Abertillery) Ltd[20]

"(1) Justices dealing with prosecutions for "causing" pollution under section 85(1) should first require the prosecution to identify what it says the defendant did to cause the pollution. If the defendant cannot be said to have done anything at all, the prosecution must fail: the defendant may have "knowingly permitted" pollution but cannot have caused it.

The prosecution need not prove that the defendant did something which was the immediate cause of the pollution: maintaining tanks, lagoons or sewage systems full of noxious liquid is doing something, even if the immediate cause of the pollution was lack of maintenance, a natural event or the act of a third party.

When the prosecution has identified something which the defendant did, the justices must decide whether it caused the pollution. They should not be diverted by questions like "What was the cause of the pollution?" or "Did something else cause the pollution?" because to say that something else caused the pollution (like brambles clogging the pumps or vandalism by third parties) is not inconsistent with the defendant having caused it as well.

If the defendant did something which produced a situation in which the polluting matter could escape but a necessary condition of the actual escape which happened was also the act of a third party or a natural event, the justices should consider whether that act or event should be regarded as a normal fact of life or something extraordinary. If it was in the general run of things a matter of ordinary occurrence, it will not negative the causal effect of the defendant's acts, even if it was not foreseeable that it would happen to that particular defendant or take that particular form. If it can be regarded as something extraordinary, it will be open to the justices to hold that the defendant did not cause the pollution.

[20] [1999] 2 AC 22

The distinction between ordinary and extraordinary is one of fact and degree to which the justices must apply their common sense and knowledge of what happens in the area."

Walker & Son (Hauliers) Ltd v Environment Agency[21]

"18. On 31 January the Judge ruled that a jury would need to consider three matters (p.6B-6F of the Ruling):

(1) Did the Company have knowledge of waste operations occurring on their land?

(2) If so, did the Company permit, i.e. allow or fail to prevent, those waste operations?

(3) Were the waste operations of which the Company had knowledge in accordance with an environmental permit?"

...

"29. ... The words 'knowingly' and 'permit' relate to knowledge of the facts and not as to the existence and scope of the permission or conditions of a licence. The Prosecution does not have to show that a defendant knew that the matters of which it was aware were not permitted. There are good reasons for this: there are means of checking the existence and conditions of environmental permits, and ignorance of these matters should not be a defence to an environmental offence."

...

"37. We have therefore concluded that the Judge was correct in his conclusion as to the proper interpretation of Regulation 38(1); and accordingly the appeal is dismissed."

---

[21] [2014] EWCA Crim 100; [2014] 4 All E.R. 825; [2014] Env. L.R. 22

Stone v Environment Agency[22]

> "46. I recognise that *Alphcell Ltd v Woodward* (above) was dealing with the 'active' limb of the offence (i.e. that which penalised 'causing' pollution), but its commentary on the purpose of including both the 'active' and the 'passive' (i.e. 'knowingly permitting') limb is instructive. Walker was dealing with a rather different point, but nonetheless the Court of Appeal endorsed Judge Lea's direction to the jury which included the alternative of failing to prevent the waste operation. Again, I have come to the clear conclusion that Mr Ostrowski's submissions are to be preferred. The Magistrates were right that the prosecution did not have to prove that the prosecution took a positive act within the period covered by the charges."

Express Ltd (t/a Express Dairies Distribution) v Environment Agency[23]

> "14. It is worth noting the context in which Lord Hoffmann used the term "extraordinary". It was in the context of it being "a necessary condition of the actual escape which happened that there be the act of a third party or a natural event", and he went on to say that Justices should consider whether that act or event should be regarded as a normal fact of life or something extraordinary. He was, therefore, addressing what in other contexts might be described as an ultroneous cause of an eventual outcome.
>
> 15. In this particular case, everything that happened flowed from the operation of this tanker on that road. That was obviously something which the appellants had done. Any vehicle's tyre may blow out. Blow outs, though thankfully rare, are certainly capable of being regarded as events in the ordinary run of things. Everything else that led to the escape of the milk from the tanker was part of the operation of that tanker on the road, and the entry of the escaped milk into the brook was

---

[22] [2018] Env. L.R. 32

[23] [2004] 1 W.L.R. 579; [2003] Env. L.R. 29

> finally caused by the driver pulling to the side of the road in that particular place.
>
> 16. In my judgment, in those circumstances, it is quite impossible to say that the chain of causation from start to finish was broken and that the principle adumbrated by Lord Hoffmann in the *Empress* case might operate to defeat that. This is a much stronger case than the *Empress* case, where there was indeed doubt about whether it was some act of a third party which had led to the escape of the liquid."

Knowingly cause

Although the word "knowingly" appears before cause in Regulation 38(1)(b) of the Environmental Permitting (England and Wales) Regulations 2016, it is not understood that this drafting makes any difference in practice. The wording in Regulation 12 of the same Regulations reflects the transposition of previous legislation relating to water discharges but it is not understood that it is intended to draw any form of practical distinction between causing a water discharge activity and causing a breach of a condition of an environmental permit. Indeed, such a distinction would be hard to rationalise in practice, even taking into account the comments of Lord Wilberforce in *Alphacell Ltd v Woodward.*

That said, the lack of the word "knowingly" was found in *R (on the application of Thames Water Utilities Ltd) v Bromley Magistrates' Court*[24] (below) to provide justification for including an unknown and unintended escape of waste within the meaning of the word "deposit".

[24] [2013] 1 W.L.R. 3641; [2013] Env. L.R. 25

Deposit

R (on the application of Thames Water Utilities Ltd) v Bromley Magistrates' Court[25]

> "25. For my part, first, as a matter of dictionary definition, I do not think it is necessary to look beyond the definition of "deposit" used by the district judge, viz "put, place(d) or set down".
>
> 26. Secondly, I readily accept the observation of Aikens LJ in Milton Keynes District Council v Fuller [2011] Env LR 641, para 39, that "deposit" is an "ordinary and uncomplicated English word". In that case, the justices had concluded that the movement of waste, previously tipped by others in the entrance to the respondents' field, did not amount to a "deposit", within section 33(1)(a) of the Act. This court held that no question of law was involved in the interpretation of the word "deposit"; on the facts, the justices' conclusion was "perfectly reasonable": para 39. As Aikens LJ went on to observe: "We cannot impose our own exegesis on the meaning of the word and then apply our meaning to the facts as found by the justices".
>
> 27. Thirdly, in the light of it being an ordinary English word, the question for this court is whether an unintended escape falls within a reasonable range of meanings for "deposit"; if yes, then there is no basis for interfering with the district judge's conclusion; if no, then the district judge's conclusion cannot stand.
>
> 28. Fourthly, I am not at all persuaded that this question can be resolved either way on the basis of the word "deposit" considered in isolation. There is something to be said for the arguments of each party and neither party's case can be disposed of merely on the basis of a dictionary definition. (1) I

[25] [2013] 1 W.L.R. 3641; [2013] Env. L.R. 25

acknowledge some attraction in Mr Tromans's submission that, inherent in the meaning of the word "deposit" is the common denominator of doing something intentionally. Further, he can properly derive a degree of assistance from the judgment of this court in the Remet Co Ltd case [1981] RTR 502 , albeit that a different statute was under consideration. (2) Conversely, it can fairly be said that Mr Harris derives support from Waite LJ's observations in Scott's case [1995] RTR 327 (para 24 above), namely, that the word is one of wide connotation, likely to attract "shades of meaning". Moreover, as will become apparent, I regard the dicta of Carnwath LJ in R (Thames Water Utilities Ltd) v Bromley Magistrates' Court (Water Services Regulation Authority intervening) [2009] 1 WLR 1247 as of significant persuasive authority. (3) Without, with respect, in any way casting doubt upon it, I am not persuaded that the judgment of Laws LJ in the Gateway case [2004] Env LR 874 advances the argument; it is one thing to conclude that escape does not extend to deliberate dumping and that deliberate dumping comes within the meaning of section 33(1)(a) of the Act; it does not at all follow that "deposit" in section 33(1)(a) does not extend to an unintended escape."

<u>Submit ... to any listed operation</u>

Listed operations are to be found in Annex I and Annex II to the Waste Framework Directive 2008/98/EC:

ANNEX I
DISPOSAL OPERATIONS

D 1 Deposit into or on to land (e.g. landfill, etc.)

D 2 Land treatment (e.g. biodegradation of liquid or sludgy discards in soils, etc.)

D 3 Deep injection (e.g. injection of pumpable discards into wells, salt domes or naturally occurring repositories, etc.)

D 4 Surface impoundment (e.g. placement of liquid or sludgy discards into pits, ponds or lagoons, etc.)

D 5 Specially engineered landfill (e.g. placement into lined discrete cells which are capped and isolated from one another and the environment, etc.)

D 6 Release into a water body except seas/oceans

D 7 Release to seas/oceans including sea-bed insertion

D 8 Biological treatment not specified elsewhere in this Annex which results in final compounds or mixtures which are discarded by means of any of the operations numbered D 1 to D 12

D 9 Physico-chemical treatment not specified elsewhere in this Annex which results in final compounds or mixtures which are discarded by means of any of the operations numbered D 1 to D 12 (e.g. evaporation, drying, calcination, etc.)

D 10 Incineration on land

D 11 Incineration at sea (*)

D 12 Permanent storage (e.g. emplacement of containers in a mine, etc.)

D 13 Blending or mixing prior to submission to any of the operations numbered D 1 to D 12 (**)

D 14 Repackaging prior to submission to any of the operations numbered D 1 to D 13

D 15 Storage pending any of the operations numbered D 1 to D 14 (excluding temporary storage, pending collection, on the site where the waste is produced) (***)

(*) This operation is prohibited by EU legislation and international conventions.

(**) If there is no other D code appropriate, this can include preliminary operations prior to disposal including pre-processing such as, inter alia, sorting, crushing, compacting, pelletising, drying, shredding, conditioning or separating prior to submission to any of the operations numbered D1 to D12.

(***) Temporary storage means preliminary storage according to point (10) of Article 3.

ANNEX II
RECOVERY OPERATIONS

R 1 Use principally as a fuel or other means to generate energy (*)

R 2 Solvent reclamation/regeneration

R 3 Recycling/reclamation of organic substances which are not used as solvents (including composting and other biological transformation processes) (**)

R 4 Recycling/reclamation of metals and metal compounds

R 5 Recycling/reclamation of other inorganic materials (***)

R 6 Regeneration of acids or bases

R 7 Recovery of components used for pollution abatement

R 8 Recovery of components from catalysts

R 9 Oil re-refining or other reuses of oil

R 10 Land treatment resulting in benefit to agriculture or ecological improvement

R 11 Use of waste obtained from any of the operations numbered R 1 to R 10

R 12 Exchange of waste for submission to any of the operations numbered R 1 to R 11 (****)

R 13 Storage of waste pending any of the operations numbered R 1 to R 12 (excluding temporary storage, pending collection, on the site where the waste is produced) (*****)

(*) This includes incineration facilities dedicated to the processing of municipal solid waste only where their energy efficiency is equal to or above:
— 0,60 for installations in operation and permitted in accordance with applicable Community legislation before 1 January 2009,
— 0,65 for installations permitted after 31 December 2008,
using the following formula:
Energy efficiency = (Ep - (Ef + Ei))/(0,97 . (Ew + Ef))
In which:
Ep means annual energy produced as heat or electricity. It is calculated with energy in the form of electricity being multiplied by 2,6 and heat produced for commercial use multiplied by 1,1 (GJ/year)
Ef means annual energy input to the system from fuels contributing to the production of steam (GJ/year)
Ew means annual energy contained in the treated waste calculated using the net calorific value of the waste (GJ/year)
Ei means annual energy imported excluding Ew and Ef (GJ/year)
0,97 is a factor accounting for energy losses due to bottom ash and radiation.
This formula shall be applied in accordance with the reference document on Best Available Techniques for waste incineration.

(**) This includes gasification and pyrolisis using the components as chemicals.

(***) This includes soil cleaning resulting in recovery of the soil and recycling of inorganic construction materials.

(****) If there is no other R code appropriate, this can include preliminary operations prior to recovery including pre-processing such as, inter alia, dismantling, sorting, crushing, compacting, pelletising, drying, shredding, conditioning, repackaging, separating, blending or mixing prior to submission to any of the operations numbered R1 to R11.

(*****) Temporary storage means preliminary storage according to point (10) of Article 3.

Storage

Skipaway Ltd v Environment Agency[26]

"32. I think it clear that waste is stored within the meaning of this condition once it has been deposited on the site and until it is removed. Mr Jones submitted that the times laid down in condition 3.6 fell to be extended by any period of operations on waste, e.g. while it was sorted. That is to my mind an unlikely and impractical interpretation. In my judgment "stored" has the same meaning in conditions 3.3 and 3.4. By way of example, there is good reason to keep the height of waste below the specified limit even while it is sorted or otherwise the subject of processing, so as to minimise or prevent its escape from the site. I see no good reason why waste that is being stored should be considered to cease to be so if an employee works at that waste seeking to sort one kind of material from another."

[26] [2006] Env. L.R. 41

Treat, keep or dispose in a manner likely to cause pollution of the environment or harm to human health

The phrase "pollution of the environment" is defined at s.29(3) of the Environmental Protection Act 1990:

> (3) *"Pollution of the environment"* means pollution of the environment due to the release or escape (into any environmental medium) from—
>
> (a) the land on which controlled waste or extractive waste is treated,
>
> (b) the land on which controlled waste or extractive waste is kept,
>
> (c) the land in or on which controlled waste or extractive waste is deposited,
>
> (d) fixed plant by means of which controlled waste or extractive waste is treated, kept or disposed of,
>
> of substances or articles constituting or resulting from the waste and capable (by reason of the quantity or concentrations involved) of causing harm to man or any other living organisms supported by the environment.

Pollution of the environment must therefore be due to the release or escape of substances or articles constituting or resulting from the waste itself and must be capable of causing harm to man or any other living organisms supported by the environment. Arguably, this definition excludes impact on amenity. The release or escape must be from the land on which the waste is treated, kept or deposited or from fixed plant by which the waste is treated, kept or disposed of. Arguably, this suggests that something more than pollution of the land itself on which the waste is kept, treated or deposited is required – the polluting effects must be as a consequence of a release or escape from that land.

Exempt waste operations

Section 33(1)(a) does not apply to an operation which falls within a description in Part 5 of Schedule 3 of the Environmental Permitting (England and Wales) Regulations 2016 and meets the conditions specified in that Part for that description. There are numerous various possible exempt waste operations, numbered U1 to U16 (Use of waste), T1 to T33 (Treatment of Waste), D1 to D8 (Deposit and limited burning of waste) and S1 to S3 (Storage of waste).

Such waste operations must be registered with the Environment Agency, together with the establishment or undertaking in relation to it and the type and quantity of waste submitted to the waste operation and the method of disposal or recovery must be consistent with the need to attain the objectives mentioned in Article 13 of the Waste Framework Directive (Schedule 2 to the Environmental Permitting (England and Wales) Regulations 2016, paragraph 4).

Article 13 reads:

Article 13
Protection of human health and the environment

> Member States shall take the necessary measures to ensure that waste management is carried out without endangering human health, without harming the environment and, in particular:
>
> (a) without risk to water, air, soil, plants or animals;
>
> (b) without causing a nuisance through noise or odours; and
>
> (c) without adversely affecting the countryside or places of special interest.

Mustafa v Environment Agency[27]

"69. In this case, to make good the charge in the indictment, the Environment Agency had to prove that, in the relevant period, the company was operating a "regulated facility" rather than an "exempt facility". If at any time during that period, the operation was not an "exempt facility" the company committed the alleged offence.

70. On a straightforward interpretation of the legislative provisions, in our view, a waste operation will only be an "exempt facility" if it fully meets the requirements of paragraph 3(1) of Schedule 2. If it does not meet those requirements in full, it cannot be an "exempt facility", and it must be a "regulated facility"; there is no other status it can then have. And if, as a "regulated facility", it is operated without an environmental permit, there is a breach of regulation 12, and an offence under regulation 38 has been committed. That, it seems to us, is this case.

71. The "requirements" that have to be met for an operation to be an "exempt waste operation", and thus an "exempt facility", are clearly set out in paragraph 3(1) of Schedule 2. There are three of them: first, that the operation satisfies "the general and specific conditions" specified in Part 1 of Schedule 3 for the relevant description of the operation (paragraph 3(1)(a); and chapter 2, section 1 , paragraph 3 and paragraph 6(3) of Schedule 3); second, that it is registered (paragraph 3(1)(b) of Schedule 2); and third, that the type and quantity of waste, and method of disposal or recovery, are consistent with the relevant objectives of the Waste Framework Directive – that it does not endanger human health or harm the environment (paragraph 3(1)(c) of Schedule 2).

72. Those three requirements are mandatory, and cumulative. None of them is said to be optional or discretionary. None of

[27] [2020] EWCA Crim 597

> them is said to override or displace the other two. They must all be satisfied. If any of them is not met, or ceases to be met, the operation cannot be an "exempt waste operation", and thus cannot be an "exempt facility" (regulation 5), but can only be a "regulated facility" (regulation 8)."

Other exceptions

Part 5 of Schedule 3 to the Environmental Permitting (England and Wales) Regulations 2016 identifies other waste operations to which section 33(1)(a) of the Environmental Protection Act 1990 does not apply. These include the temporary storage of waste at the place of production, the temporary storage of waste at a place controlled by the producer and the temporary storage of waste at a collection point. Each of these waste operations is subject to specific conditions, although there is no obligation to register these waste operations with the Environment Agency.

The form of the charges

R v Leighton (Ian)[28]

> "Section 33(1) of the 1990 Act provides:
>
> "(1). . . a person shall not
>
> (a) deposit controlled waste, or knowingly cause or knowingly permit controlled waste to be deposited in or on any land unless a waste management licence authorising the deposit is in force and the deposit is in accordance with the licence;
>
> (b) treat, keep or dispose of controlled waste, or knowingly cause or knowingly permit controlled waste to be treated, kept or disposed of—

[28] [1997] Env. L.R. 411

(i) in or on any land,

(ii) by means of any mobile plant, except under and in accordance with a waste management licence;

(c) treat, keep or dispose of controlled waste in a manner likely to cause pollution of the environment or harm to human health."

In our view, that provision creates, in paragraphs (a), (b) and (c), three separate offences, each of which may be committed by any one of the different acts specified.

Accordingly, in each case it was in principle permissible for the prosecution to charge a single offence stating the various acts of commission in the alternative. To have required it to charge each alternative in a separate count would have resulted in a prolix and unmanageable indictment. We say "in principle" only to make the point that if, in any instance, the prosecution is confident before trial that it can prove the precise mode of committing the offence and/or that it cannot prove one or more of the others, it should specify the particular mode upon which it relies and leave it at that. There would be no point in including alternatives provided by the statute for which there is no evidential support. However, in our view, the nature of the prosecution case here justified the prosecution pleading and relying on the various alternatives. Although Leighton asserted in interview that he was closely involved in the management of the site, he did not accept responsibility in any clear way for any of the alleged contraventions, and at the trial the main thrust of his evidence was to distance the Company and himself from the day to day conduct of the site."

Onus of proof

Under s.33(1)(a), an offence is committed "unless an environmental permit authorising the deposit is in force and the deposit is in accordance with the permit". In *Environment Agency v M E Foley (Contractors) Ltd*[29] the issue was whether the waste did or did not contain more than 10 per cent of a particular chemical compound, in which case its deposit would have fallen outwith the environmental waste management licence. The onus of proof was held to lie with the Environment Agency.

Deposit from motor vehicles

Environment Agency v Melland[30]

> "16. In my judgment, evidence of ownership of a vehicle is capable of amounting to prima facie evidence that the owner controls, or is in a position to control, the vehicle. I stress the words "is capable of" amounting to prima facie evidence because there may be evidence before the court that, at the material time, the vehicle had been stolen or that it had been loaned to another or that it was a hired vehicle. If, for instance, the owner was Hertz or Avis or some other well-known hire company, the court would be entitled to decline to draw the inference that ownership carried with it the ability to control the vehicle.
>
> 17. Each case will turn on its own facts. The facts of this case are that the owner or keeper of the vehicle at the material times was the respondent, Mr Melland, who traded as Melland Skip Hire, and that the waste was deposited from the vehicle by means of a skip. In my view, that evidence constituted prima facie evidence from which it could properly be inferred that the respondent controlled, or was in a position to control, the vehicle at the material times. It therefore constituted sufficient evidence upon which to convict the respondent in the absence of any evidence from him that he did not control, or was not in a position to control, the vehicle."

[29] [2002] Env. L.R. 27
[30] [2002] Env. L.R. 29

Defences

It should be noted that there exists a due diligence defence under s.33(7) of the Environmental Protection Act 1990 that does not exist within the Environmental Permitting (England and Wales) Regulations 2016. The removal of this defence was a deliberate decision and the subject of some debate before the original draft of the Environmental Permitting Regulations was brought into force.

A prosecuting authority that seeks to amend an indictment in order to reframe a charge under the Environmental Permitting (England and Wales) Regulations 2016 so as to deprive a defendant of a due diligence defence may be susceptible to an abuse of process argument on the grounds that this is an unjustifiable manipulation of the Court's process.

The only specific defence that is common to both sets of legislation is that of emergency.

Directions to a jury

R v W[31]

> "34. We conclude, like the Court of Appeal in Northern Ireland, that excavated soil which has to be discarded by the then "holder" is capable of being waste within the Act and, in any individual case, ordinarily will be. Having become waste it remains waste unless something happens to alter that. Whether such an event has happened is a question of fact for the jury. The possibility of re-use at some indefinite future time does not alter its status: see *Palin Granit*, and indeed *ARCO*. Actual re-use may do so (*Inglenorth*), but only if consistent with the aims and objectives of the Act and of the Directive: (c.f. *O'Hare*), the principal ones of which are the avoidance of harm to persons or to the environment, as set out in the recitals

[31] [2010] Env. L.R. 41

to the Directive. Which of those aims and objectives are relevant to an individual case will depend on the cases presented by the parties. In this case, for example, the main concern maintained by the Crown is for the environment around the village where the respondents' farm lies (as a Special Area of Conservation) and visual amenity in the area generally. Matters which, in our judgement, are readily capable of assessment by a jury in deciding whether any material in issue is in fact "waste"."

R v Jones (Evan)[32]

The correct analysis of the position in respect of the offence under s.33 was that contained in *R v W [2010] Env. L.R. 41* . This was that, at the moment at which B was on the point of depositing material on C's land, the conduct of B in bringing the material to that point, coupled with the purpose of C in receiving the material was capable of bringing about a change in the status of the material for the purpose of the relevant statutory regime so that, at that moment, the material ceased to be waste subject to the nature of the material and the nature of the intended reuse and its environmental impact. An intention of immediate re-use did not provide an automatic defence to a charge under s.33(3) but depended on the nature of the material and the intended reuse of it. The court in *R v W* held that where B delivered material which was waste, to C for C's immediate use, the deposit was not necessarily waste. That would depend on the nature of the material, the intended re-use, and whether it was compatible with environmental objectives in the Waste Directives and domestic legislation. It had not found that a deposit by B was necessarily unlawful. In the present case, the effect of the judge's direction on waste had been that the deposit by B on C's land was necessarily unlawful. That amounted to a fundamental misdirection as to the statutory requirements of an offence pursuant to s.33 , and that had not been cured by his further directions.

[32] [2012] Env. L.R. D2

R v Jagger (Michael Edward)[33]

"30. Considering the written definition of waste provided to the jury, we note that at [3] the judge stated that material remained controlled waste unless something happened to alter that. The judge did not then go on to assist the jury in any way by reference to the facts of this case by indicating to them factors which might have a bearing on the question of whether such altercation had taken place. We also note that at [4] the judge referred to the possibility that material was not controlled waste if it had been acceptably recovered or disposed of. Again there was no reference to what that might mean in the context of this case. It seems to us that it was far from self-evident what that phrase meant.

…

33. We do not underestimate the task of the judge in this case. He had other defendants to deal with and a number of other issues to cover in relation to them, as well as those pertaining to the appellant's case. As has previously been observed, this is not a straightforward area of the law, and the question of what is waste at any given time is not clear-cut. This perhaps underlines the need for a judge to give the jury sufficient directions on what is a fact-sensitive decision. We have come to the conclusion that there is considerable force in the argument that as a result of his understandable desire to keep the case simple for the jury, the judge oversimplified his directions to the detriment of the appellant's case. The effect of this was unduly to restrict the jury's consideration of valid arguments available to the appellant on the question of waste. The result was that he was deprived of fair consideration by the jury of a significant issue."

[33] [2015] Env. L.R. 25

CHAPTER SIX

WATER POLLUTION

Reg 38 Environmental Permitting (England and Wales) Regulations 2016

38.— Offences

(1) It is an offence for a person to—

(a) contravene regulation 12(1) …

Reg 12 Environmental Permitting (England and Wales) Regulations 2016

12.— Requirement for an environmental permit

(1) A person must not, except under and to the extent authorised by an environmental permit—

(a) operate a regulated facility, or

(b) cause or knowingly permit a water discharge activity or groundwater activity.

Cause or knowingly permit

Alphacell Ltd v Woodward[34]

"The subsection evidently contemplates two things—causing, which must involve some active operation or chain of operations involving as the result the pollution of the stream;

[34] [1972] A.C. 824; [1972] 2 W.L.R. 1320; [1972] 2 All E.R. 475

knowingly permitting, which involves a failure to prevent the pollution, which failure, however, must be accompanied by knowledge. I see no reason either for reading back the word "knowingly" into the first limb, or for reading the first limb as, by deliberate contrast, hitting something which is unaccompanied by knowledge. The first limb involves causing and this is what has to be interpreted.

In my opinion, "causing" here must be given a common sense meaning and I deprecate the introduction of refinements, such as causa causans, effective cause or novus actus. There may be difficulties where acts of third persons or natural forces are concerned but I find the present case comparatively simple. The appellants abstract water, pass it through their works where it becomes polluted, conduct it to a settling tank communicating directly with the stream, into which the polluted water will inevitably overflow if the level rises over the overflow point. They plan, however, to recycle the water by pumping it back from the settling tank into their works: if the pumps work properly this will happen and the level in the tank will remain below the overflow point. It did not happen on the relevant occasion due to some failure in the pumps.

In my opinion, this is a clear case of causing the polluted water to enter the stream. The whole complex operation which might lead to this result was an operation deliberately conducted by the appellants and I fail to see how a defect in one stage of it, even if we must assume that this happened without their negligence, can enable them to say they did not cause the pollution. In my opinion, complication of this case by infusion of the concept of mens rea, and its exceptions, is unnecessary and undesirable. The section is clear, its application plain. I agree with the majority of the Divisional Court, who upheld the conviction, except that rather than say that the actions of the appellants were a cause of the pollution I think it more accurate to say that the appellants caused the polluting matter to enter the stream."

Environment Agency v Empress Car Co. (Abertillery) Ltd[35]

> "(1) Justices dealing with prosecutions for "causing" pollution under section 85(1) should first require the prosecution to identify what it says the defendant did to cause the pollution. If the defendant cannot be said to have done anything at all, the prosecution must fail: the defendant may have "knowingly permitted" pollution but cannot have caused it.
>
> The prosecution need not prove that the defendant did something which was the immediate cause of the pollution: maintaining tanks, lagoons or sewage systems full of noxious liquid is doing something, even if the immediate cause of the pollution was lack of maintenance, a natural event or the act of a third party.
>
> When the prosecution has identified something which the defendant did, the justices must decide whether it caused the pollution. They should not be diverted by questions like "What was the cause of the pollution?" or "Did something else cause the pollution?" because to say that something else caused the pollution (like brambles clogging the pumps or vandalism by third parties) is not inconsistent with the defendant having caused it as well.
>
> If the defendant did something which produced a situation in which the polluting matter could escape but a necessary condition of the actual escape which happened was also the act of a third party or a natural event, the justices should consider whether that act or event should be regarded as a normal fact of life or something extraordinary. If it was in the general run of things a matter of ordinary occurrence, it will not negative the causal effect of the defendant's acts, even if it was not foreseeable that it would happen to that particular defendant or take that particular form. If it can be regarded as something extraordinary, it will be open to the justices to hold that the defendant did not cause the pollution.

[35] [1999] 2 AC 22

The distinction between ordinary and extraordinary is one of fact and degree to which the justices must apply their common sense and knowledge of what happens in the area."

Walker & Son (Hauliers) Ltd v Environment Agency[36]

"18. On 31 January the Judge ruled that a jury would need to consider three matters (p.6B-6F of the Ruling):

(1) Did the Company have knowledge of waste operations occurring on their land?

(2) If so, did the Company permit, i.e. allow or fail to prevent, those waste operations?

(3) Were the waste operations of which the Company had knowledge in accordance with an environmental permit?"

...

"29. ... The words 'knowingly' and 'permit' relate to knowledge of the facts and not as to the existence and scope of the permission or conditions of a licence. The Prosecution does not have to show that a defendant knew that the matters of which it was aware were not permitted. There are good reasons for this: there are means of checking the existence and conditions of environmental permits, and ignorance of these matters should not be a defence to an environmental offence."

...

"37. We have therefore concluded that the Judge was correct in his conclusion as to the proper interpretation of Regulation 38(1); and accordingly the appeal is dismissed."

[36] [2014] EWCA Crim 100; [2014] 4 All E.R. 825; [2014] Env.L.R. 22

Stone v Environment Agency[37]

> "46. I recognise that Alphcell Ltd v Woodward (above) was dealing with the 'active' limb of the offence (i.e. that which penalised 'causing' pollution), but its commentary on the purpose of including both the 'active' and the 'passive' (i.e. 'knowingly permitting') limb is instructive. Walker was dealing with a rather different point, but nonetheless the Court of Appeal endorsed Judge Lea's direction to the jury which included the alternative of failing to prevent the waste operation. Again, I have come to the clear conclusion that Mr Ostrowski's submissions are to be preferred. The Magistrates were right that the prosecution did not have to prove that the prosecution took a positive act within the period covered by the charges."

Express Ltd (t/a Express Dairies Distribution) v Environment Agency[38]

> "14. It is worth noting the context in which Lord Hoffmann used the term "extraordinary". It was in the context of it being "a necessary condition of the actual escape which happened that there be the act of a third party or a natural event", and he went on to say that Justices should consider whether that act or event should be regarded as a normal fact of life or something extraordinary. He was, therefore, addressing what in other contexts might be described as an ultroneous cause of an eventual outcome.
>
> 15. In this particular case, everything that happened flowed from the operation of this tanker on that road. That was obviously something which the appellants had done. Any vehicle's tyre may blow out. Blow outs, though thankfully rare, are certainly capable of being regarded as events in the ordinary run of things. Everything else that led to the escape of the milk from the tanker was part of the operation of that tanker on the road, and the entry of the escaped milk into the brook was

---

37 [2018] Env. L.R. 32

38 [2004] 1 W.L.R. 579; [2003] Env. L.R. 29

> finally caused by the driver pulling to the side of the road in that particular place.
>
> 16. In my judgment, in those circumstances, it is quite impossible to say that the chain of causation from start to finish was broken and that the principle adumbrated by Lord Hoffmann in the *Empress* case might operate to defeat that. This is a much stronger case than the *Empress* case, where there was indeed doubt about whether it was some act of a third party which had led to the escape of the liquid."

Control

Noticeably absent from the discussion in *Empress Cars* is the extent to which an operator must be in a position in which to be able to exercise control over where the cause of the pollution occurred. An obvious example would be where trade effluent from a factory premises escapes into the local watercourse as a result of a leak in pipework outside of the premises of the factory and under the control (and ownership) of another, for example the water utility company. It is strongly arguable that the business operating the factory has done nothing in those circumstances to 'cause' the pollution, despite the fact that 'but for' the operation if the business, no trade effluent would have entered the watercourse. Some form of control should be exercisable over the waste by the defendant at the physical point where the discharge took place.

In *Empress* itself Lord Hoffman found that, at [399], "*...The company maintained a diesel tank in a yard which drained directly into the river...*". Then further at [401], and considering past cases, "...[T]*he pollution was caused by something which the defendants did. Maintaining lagoons of effluent*[39] *or operating the municipal sewage system is doing something.*[40]". Both of the foregoing quotations necessarily imply some control over the waste/noxious liquid, whether by maintenance or operation, to enable causation to be established for the purposes of s.85(1) of the Water Resources Act 1991.

---

[39] *Price* v *Cromack* [1975] 1 W.L.R. 988

[40] *Wychavon District Council* v *National Rivers Authority* [1993] 1 W.L.R. 125

Further examples of cases where control must be a necessary element for establishing causation are:

Alphacell Ltd v *Woodward*[41] in which settling tanks at a paper factory overflowed into a river where the pumps were blocked by brambles and ferns: the maintenance of the pumps was within the control of the defendant company;

CPC (UK) Ltd. v *National Rivers Authority*[42] in which a factory operator was held to have caused pollutant to have entered controlled waters because of a fractured pipe, where the pipe was within their control;

Express Ltd v *Environment Agency*[43] in which the defendant allowed its premises to be used to transfer cream from an outside supplier to one of its customers, during which some of the cream ended up in a brook: the method of transferring the cream was within the control of the defendant.

S.121 Water Industry Act 1991

121.— Conditions of consent.

(1) The power of a sewerage undertaker, on an application under section 119 above, to give a consent with respect to the discharge of any trade effluent shall be a power to give a consent either unconditionally or subject to such conditions as the sewerage undertaker thinks fit to impose with respect to—

(a) the sewer or sewers into which the trade effluent may be discharged;

(b) the nature or composition of the trade effluent which may be discharged;

---

41 [1972] AC 824

42 [1995] Env. L.R. 131

43 [2005] Env. L.R. 7

(c) the maximum quantity of trade effluent which may be discharged on any one day, either generally or into a particular sewer; and

(d) the highest rate at which trade effluent may be discharged, either generally or into a particular sewer.

(2) Conditions with respect to all or any of the following matters may also be attached under this section to a consent to the discharge of trade effluent from any trade premises—

(a) the period or periods of the day during which the trade effluent may be discharged from the trade premises into the sewer;

(b) the exclusion from the trade effluent of all condensing water;

(c) the elimination or diminution, in cases falling within subsection (3) below, of any specified constituent of the trade effluent, before it enters the sewer;

(d) the temperature of the trade effluent at the time when it is discharged into the sewer, and its acidity or alkalinity at that time;

(e) the payment by the occupier of the trade premises to the undertaker of charges for the reception of the trade effluent into the sewer and for the disposal of the effluent;

(f) the provision and maintenance of such an inspection chamber or manhole as will enable a person readily to take samples, at any time, of what is passing into the sewer from the trade premises;
(g) the provision, testing and maintenance of such meters as may be required to measure the volume and rate of discharge

of any trade effluent being discharged from the trade premises into the sewer;

(h) the provision, testing and maintenance of apparatus for determining the nature and composition of any trade effluent being discharged from the premises into the sewer;

(i) the keeping of records of the volume, rate of discharge, nature and composition of any trade effluent being discharged and, in particular, the keeping of records of readings of meters and other recording apparatus provided in compliance with any other condition attached to the consent; and

(j) the making of returns and giving of other information to the sewerage undertaker concerning the volume, rate of discharge, nature and composition of any trade effluent discharged from the trade premises into the sewer.

(3) A case falls within this subsection where the sewerage undertaker is satisfied that the constituent in question, either alone or in combination with any matter with which it is likely to come into contact while passing through any sewers-

(a) would injure or obstruct those sewers, or make the treatment or disposal of the sewage from those sewers specially difficult or expensive; or

(b) in the case of trade effluent which is to be or is discharged—

(i) into a sewer having an outfall in any harbour or tidal water; or

(ii) into a sewer which connects directly or indirectly with a sewer or sewage disposal works having such an outfall,

would cause or tend to cause injury or obstruction to the navigation on, or the use of, the harbour or tidal water.

(4) In the exercise of the power conferred by virtue of subsection (2)(e) above, regard shall be had—

(a) to the nature and composition and to the volume and rate of discharge of the trade effluent discharged;

(b) to any additional expense incurred or likely to be incurred by a sewerage undertaker in connection with the reception or disposal of the trade effluent; and

(c) to any revenue likely to be derived by the undertaker from the trade effluent.

(5) If, in the case of any trade premises, a condition imposed under this section is contravened, the occupier of the premises shall be guilty of an offence and liable—

(a) on summary conviction, to a fine not exceeding the statutory maximum; and

(b) on conviction on indictment, to a fine.

(6) In this section *"harbour"* and *"tidal water"* have the same meanings as in the Merchant Shipping Act 1995.

(7) This section has effect subject to the provisions of sections 133 and 135(3) below.

In force: 1 January 1996

Discharge consents

Conditions imposed by sewerage undertakers on discharges to the sewers that they control are generally determined so that the sewage undertaker will meet its obligations for discharge from the receiving treatment works.

In light of the significant penalties that can be imposed on sewerage undertakers for pollution offences, principally due to the very high turnover of such companies, it can be expected that a firmer and firmer line will be taken by sewerage undertakers to those that breach their discharge consents. Sewerage undertakers do take enforcement action against companies that breach their consent. In addition, increasing pressure and legal obligations to improve water quality will only lead to increased tightening of consents to discharge.

Although section 121 is not directly referred to in the Sentencing Guideline, in the view of the authors there is no reason in principle why the same sentencing approach, if not the same starting points for sentence, would not apply to such cases.

S.111 Water Industry Act 1991

111.— Restrictions on use of public sewers.

(1) Subject to the provisions of Chapter III of this Part, no person shall throw, empty or turn, or suffer or permit to be thrown or emptied or to pass, into any public sewer, or into any drain or sewer communicating with a public sewer—

(a) any matter likely to injure the sewer or drain, to interfere with the free flow of its contents or to affect prejudicially the treatment and disposal of its contents; or

(b) any such chemical refuse or waste steam, or any such liquid of a temperature higher than forty-three degrees Celsius, as by virtue of subsection (2) below is a prohibited substance; or

(c) any petroleum spirit or carbide of calcium.

(2) For the purposes of subsection (1) above, chemical refuse, waste steam or a liquid of a temperature higher than that mentioned in that subsection is a prohibited substance if (either alone or in combination with the contents of the sewer or drain

in question) it is or, in the case of the liquid, is when so heated—

(a) dangerous;

(b) the cause of a nuisance; or

(c) injurious, or likely to cause injury, to health.

(3) A person who contravenes any of the provisions of this section shall be guilty of an offence and liable—

(a) on summary conviction, to a fine not exceeding the statutory maximum and to a further fine not exceeding £50 for each day on which the offence continues after conviction;

(b) on conviction on indictment, to imprisonment for a term not exceeding two years or to a fine or to both.

(4) For the purposes of so much of subsection (3) above as makes provision for the imposition of a daily penalty—

(a) the court by which a person is convicted of the original offence may fix a reasonable date from the date of conviction for compliance by the defendant with any directions given by the court; and

(b) where a court has fixed such a period, the daily penalty shall not be imposed in respect of any day before the end of that period.

(5) In this section the expression *"petroleum spirit"* means any such—

(a) crude petroleum;

(b) oil made from petroleum or from coal, shale, peat or other bituminous substances; or

(c) product of petroleum or mixture containing petroleum,
as, when tested in the manner prescribed by or under the Petroleum (Consolidation) Act 1928, gives off an inflammable vapour at a temperature of less than twenty-three degrees Celsius.

In force: 1 April 2007

Restrictions on the use of public sewers

Section 111 of the Water Industry Act 1991 is included within the list of other relevant and analogous offences found in the Definitive Sentencing Guideline for Environmental Offences. As with section 121, expect sewerage undertakers to adopt a firmer line to enforcement of this section given the significant penalties that those undertakers can face from breaches of their own environmental permits.

CHAPTER SEVEN
DUTY OF CARE

S. 34 Environmental Protection Act 1990

34.— Duty of care etc. as respects waste.

(1) Subject to subsection (2) below, it shall be the duty of any person who imports, produces, carries, keeps, treats or disposes of controlled waste or, as a dealer or broker, has control of such waste, to take all such measures applicable to him in that capacity as are reasonable in the circumstances—

(a) to prevent any contravention by any other person of section 33 above;

(aa) to prevent any contravention by any other person of regulation 12 of the Environmental Permitting Regulations or of a condition of an environmental permit;

(b) to prevent the escape of the waste from his control or that of any other person; and

(c) on the transfer of the waste, to secure

(i) that the transfer is only to an authorised person or to a person for authorised transport purposes; and

(ii) that there is transferred such a written description of the waste as will enable other persons to avoid a contravention of that section or regulation 12 of the Environmental Permitting Regulations, or a contravention of a condition of an environmental permit, and to comply with the duty under this subsection as respects the escape of waste.

(1A) It shall be the duty of any person who is responsible for the management of extractive waste to take all such measures applicable to him in that capacity as are reasonable in the circumstances—

(a) to prevent any contravention by any other person of section 33 above;

(b) to prevent any contravention by another person of regulation 12 of the 2007 Regulations or of a condition of an environmental permit; and

(c) to prevent the escape of the waste from his control or that of any other person.

(2) The duty imposed by subsection (1) above does not apply to an occupier of domestic property as respects the household waste produced on the property.

(2A) It shall be the duty of the occupier of any domestic property in England or Wales to take all such measures available to him as are reasonable in the circumstances to secure that any transfer by him of household waste produced on the property is only to an authorised person or to a person for authorised transport purposes.

(3) The following are authorised persons for the purposes of subsections (1)(c) and (2A) above—

(a) any authority which is a waste collection authority for the purposes of this Part;

(b) any person who is the holder of an environmental permit in relation to a waste operation;

(ba) any person who is carrying on an exempt waste operation;

(c) any person to whom section 33(1) above does not apply by virtue of regulations under subsection (3) of that section or by virtue of regulations under section 2 of the Pollution Prevention and Control Act 1999;

(d) any person registered as a carrier of controlled waste under section 2 of the Control of Pollution (Amendment) Act 1989;

(e) any person who is not required to be so registered by virtue of regulations under section 1(3) of that Act; and

(f) a waste disposal authority in Scotland.

(3A) The Secretary of State may by regulations amend subsection (3) above so as to add, whether generally or in such circumstances as may be prescribed in the regulations, any person specified in the regulations, or any description of person so specified, to the persons who are authorised persons for the purposes of subsections (1)(c) and (2A) above.

(4) The following are authorised transport purposes for the purposes of subsections (1)(c) and (2A) above—

(a) the transport of controlled waste within the same premises between different places in those premises;

(b) the transport to a place in Great Britain of controlled waste which has been brought from a country or territory outside Great Britain not having been landed in Great Britain until it arrives at that place; and

(c) the transport by air or sea of controlled waste from a place in Great Britain to a place outside Great Britain;
and *"transport"* has the same meaning in this subsection as in the Control of Pollution (Amendment) Act 1989.

(4A) For the purposes of subsection (1)(c)(ii) above—

(a) a transfer of waste in stages shall be treated as taking place when the first stage of the transfer takes place, and

(b) a series of transfers between the same parties of waste of the same description shall be treated as a single transfer taking place when the first of the transfers in the series takes place.

(5) The Secretary of State may, by regulations, make provision imposing requirements on any person who is subject to the duty imposed by subsection (1) above as respects the making and retention of documents and the furnishing of documents or copies of documents.

(6) Any person who fails to comply with the duty imposed by subsection (1), (1A) or (2A) above or with any requirement imposed under subsection (5) above shall be liable—

(a) on summary conviction, to a fine not exceeding the statutory maximum; and

(b) on conviction on indictment, to a fine.

(7) The Secretary of State shall, after consultation with such persons or bodies as appear to him representative of the interests concerned, prepare and issue a code of practice for the purpose of providing to persons practical guidance on how to discharge the duty imposed on them by subsection (1) above.

(8) The Secretary of State may from time to time revise a code of practice issued under subsection (7) above by revoking, amending or adding to the provisions of the code.

(9) A code of practice prepared in pursuance of subsection (7) above shall be laid.

(a) before both Houses of Parliament; or

(b) if it relates to Scotland before the Scottish Parliament.

(10) A code of practice issued under subsection (7) above shall be admissible in evidence and if any provision of such a code appears to the court to be relevant to any question arising in the proceedings it shall be taken into account in determining that question.

(11) Different codes of practice may be prepared and issued under subsection (7) above for different areas.

In force: 20 March 2019

Reg 35 Waste (England and Wales) Regulations 2011

35.— Waste information

(1) This regulation takes effect as if it were made in exercise of the power in section 34(5) of the Environmental Protection Act 1990.

(2) When controlled waste is transferred in accordance with section 34(1)(c) of that Act the written description of the waste ("written information") must—

(a) identify the waste to which it relates by reference to the appropriate codes in the List of Wastes, give a description of the waste and state—

(i) its quantity and whether it is loose or in a container,

(ii) if in a container, the kind of container,

(iii) the time and place of transfer, and

(iv) the SIC code of the transferor;

(b) give the name and address of the transferor and the transferee and be signed by them;

(c) state whether each of the transferor and transferee are—

(i) the producer of the waste,

(ii) the importer of the waste,

(iii) the transporter of the waste,

(iv) a local authority,

(v) a holder of an environmental permit under [the Environmental Permitting (England and Wales) Regulations 2016, in which case the note must include the permit number (if any),

(vi) a person carrying on an operation to which section 33(1)(a) of the Environmental Protection Act 1990 does not apply by virtue of regulation 4(3) of the Environmental Permitting (England and Wales) Regulations 2016,

(vii) a person registered as a carrier of controlled waste under the Control of Pollution (Amendment) Act 1989, in which case the note must include the registration number (if any),

(viii) a person registered as a broker of or dealer in controlled waste, in which case the note must include the registration number (if any);

(d) confirm that the transferor has discharged the duty in regulation 12.

(3) Until the end of the period of 6 months beginning with the day on which these Regulations are made, the written information may omit the matters required by paragraph (2)(a)(iv) and (d).

(4) The written information may be in electronic form if the person producing it can do so in a visible and legible documentary form.

(5) Where the written information is in electronic form, the signature required by paragraph (2)(b) must be an electronic signature (and *"electronic signature"* means data in electronic form which are attached to or logically associated with the written information and which serve as a method of authentication).

(6) The transferor and the transferee must keep the written information, or a copy of it, for at least 2 years and produce it to an officer of the appropriate body or of a waste collection authority on demand within 7 days.

(7) This regulation does not apply where the waste transferred is hazardous waste and the consignment note and, where appropriate, schedule required by the Hazardous Waste (England and Wales) Regulations 2005 or the Hazardous Waste (Wales) Regulations 2005 are completed and dealt with in accordance with those Regulations.

(8) In this regulation *"SIC code"* means a code included in the UK Standard Industrial Classification of Industrial Activities 2007 (SIC 2007) published by the Office for National Statistics on 14th December 2007

In force: 1 January 2017

General observations

DEFRA last updated the Waste Duty of Care Code of Practice on 26 November 2018. Pursuant to s.34(10) Environmental Protection Act 1990, the Code of Practice is admissible and relevant to proceedings. The Code of Practice sets out relevant guidance on the scope of the duty of care and to whom the duty of care applies. The Code of Practice can be accessed on the Gov.uk website[44].

[44] https://www.gov.uk/government/publications/waste-duty-of-care-code-of-practice#history, last accessed 16 October 2020.

Milton Keynes Council v Leisure Connection Ltd[45]

> "13. On behalf of the respondent Mr Kay submitted, correctly, that the prosecution does not have to establish that an escape has taken place for the purposes of s.34(1)(b) , it has to establish that there has been a failure to exercise the statutory duty of care, namely to take all reasonable measures to prevent the escape, see Camden LBC v Mortgage Times Group Ltd [2006] EWHC 1615 (Admin) , per Latham L.J.at [9]. In the *Camden* case there was an issue as to whether or not there had been what could properly be described as an "escape" of the waste. In the present case, on the unchallenged evidence of Ms Masters, there had been an escape of waste from the respondent's control, see the extracts from her evidence set out above which included her contention that "the rubbish was not contained and was escaping".
>
> 14. There was evidence therefore that the respondent had, for whatever reason, failed to prevent the escape of the waste from its control.
>
> 15. I accept Mr Kay's submission that it does not automatically follow from the fact that there will have been a failure to prevent an escape that there has been a failure to take all reasonable measures to prevent such an escape. Circumstances can be envisaged, for example, an escape of waste as the result of an explosion caused by the negligence or malice of a third party, where it would not be right to draw the inference that there had been a failure to take all reasonable steps to prevent an escape from the mere fact that there had been an escape. But this was not such a case. There was nothing in the evidence before the magistrates to suggest that *this* escape of waste at the back of the respondent's leisure centre could not have been prevented by the taking of reasonable measures. The mere presence of the compactor at the rear of the centre could not, on

[45] [2010] Env. L.R. 4

any rational basis, have amounted to the taking by the respondent of *all* reasonable measures to prevent the escape of waste, see para.42 of the case stated above."

Mountpace Ltd v Haringey LBC[46]

"24. This submission concentrated on the factual framework of the appellant company having contracted out the renovation works to an independent contractor, that although the appellant company was the freeholder of the premises where the waste was being generated, and the waste was being generated by works being carried out at its request under the contract, the appellant "operated" from a distant address and had no reason to know these particular transfers were being effected on the days they were, and hence on those particular days the waste was " *plainly not under the Appellant's control* " (skeleton argument [14]) or " *not as a matter of practicality under the Appellant's control* " (submission in oral argument). Mr Sonn's written submissions were that as a matter of common sense, regardless of what the appellant could have put in a lengthy written contract of appointment:

"[U]nless the appellant had employed/engaged someone to be present at the Property 24 hours a day for the duration of the renovation, it could not have prevented (the contractor) from disposing of waste unlawfully."

Only if by chance the appellant, through, for example one of its directors passing by, had been present on the site at the time of the transfers would—so the argument ran—the position have been different.

25. The argument amounts in effect to a submission that on the days in question the only waste holder who had any control or practical control over the waste was the contractor.

---

[46] [2012] Env. L.R. 32

> 26. The fallacy in this submission is that it ignores the facts that the appellant company was at all material times the producer of the waste—as found by the justices and conceded by Mr Sonn—and it was waste which was foreseeably being transferred from its own premises. Further it fails to distinguish between the question of compliance with the duty under s.34(1)(c) and questions of causation. The obligation under subs.(6) which creates the offence, is to comply with the duty under subs.(1) , and it can be no defence in the event of proof of non-compliance, that in the particular circumstances, even if the duty had been fulfilled, there would still have been a transfer to an unauthorised person."

Seaboard Offshore Ltd v Secretary of State for Transport[47] (by analogy)

> "It may very well be that in pursuance of the duty imposed by section 31 a system such as desiderated on behalf of the Secretary of State ought to be laid down by an owner, charterer or manager, and that appropriate measures should be taken to see that it is adhered to. The problem for the Secretary of State is that this does not appear to be the way in which the case was presented to the justices, so that they were not in a position to apply their minds to the question whether these were reasonable steps to be taken by the defendants to secure the safe operation of the ship and whether they failed to take them. The justices say that they found that the defendants caused the ship to be operated in an unsafe way by only allowing the chief engineer two hours and 50 minutes in which to familiarise himself with the ship before sailing. They make no finding as to how it came about that the ship sailed while that was the situation, nor as to who it was who gave the instruction to sail. They had expressed the opinion that *Tesco Supermarkets Ltd. v. Nattrass* had no application to section 31 of the Act of 1988. That was in response to a contention by the defendants that since no evidence had been adduced of any decisions taken or failed to be taken by their senior management the information

---

[47] [1994] 1 W.L.R. 541

ought to be dismissed. It seems, therefore, that the justices took the view that the defendants were criminally liable even though the putting to sea by the ship with a chief engineer insufficiently familiar with the engines was the fault of some employee of the defendants other than the senior management. That view was erroneous, and in the circumstances the conviction cannot stand.

In the judgment of the Divisional Court there is some discussion as to whether or not the offence provided for by section 31 is one of strict liability, involving no necessary element of mens rea. It is not, however, helpful to seek to categorise the offence as either being or not being one of strict liability. It consists simply in failure to take steps which by an objective standard are held to be reasonable steps to take in the interests of the safe operation of a ship, and the duty which it places on the owner, charterer or manager is a personal one. The owner, charterer or manager is criminally liable if he fails personally in the duty, but is not criminally liable for the acts or omissions of his subordinate employees if he has himself taken all such reasonable steps."

CHAPTER EIGHT

TRANSFRONTIER SHIPMENT OF WASTE

Transfrontier Shipment of Waste Regulations 2007

23. Prohibition on export of certain waste for recovery to non-OECD Decision countries

A person commits an offence if, in breach of Article 36(1), he transports waste specified in that Article that is destined for recovery in a country to which the OECD Decision does not apply.

Waste Shipment Regulation (1013/2006) Article 36

Article 36

Exports prohibition

1. Exports from the Community of the following wastes destined for recovery in countries to which the OECD Decision does not apply are prohibited:

(a) wastes listed as hazardous in Annex V;

(b) wastes listed in Annex V, Part 3;

(c) hazardous wastes not classified under one single entry in Annex V;

(d) mixtures of hazardous wastes and mixtures of hazardous wastes with non-hazardous wastes not classified under one single entry in Annex V;

> (e) wastes that the country of destination has notified to be hazardous under Article 3 of the Basel Convention;
>
> (f) wastes the import of which has been prohibited by the country of destination; or
>
> (g) wastes which the competent authority of dispatch has reason to believe will not be managed in an environmentally sound manner, as referred to in Article 49, in the country of destination concerned.

By way of comment, it is effectively impossible to eliminate contamination from waste sorted for export. Waste plastics or waste paper bales will always inevitably contain some contaminants. Contamination and the extent to which contamination can determine the type of waste being exported is therefore a very live issue in cases brought under the Transfrontier Shipment of Waste Regulations 2007.

R v Ideal Waste Paper Co Ltd[48]

> "We accept that a very high standard is required of operators in this field. We are mindful of the difficulties faced by commercial operators conducting what is an important and valuable business, not only for them but in the public interest. We are mindful of the extreme difficulty, to which reference has been made, in setting a helpful test of general application when considering and deciding what comes within the definition of household waste. We are not unmindful of the difficulties involved in juries deciding this issue. Juries are familiar with having to decide issues of fact, what evidence to accept. They are accustomed to considering the state of mind of witnesses and defendants, whether they were acting dishonestly, whether there was consent. A decision as to whether household waste has been converted into waste paper is a decision of a somewhat

[48] [2012] Env. L.R. 19

different kind from those they are normally called upon to make.

There are those who take the view that juries are not the most appropriate forum for trials in environmental cases such as this. We express no view about that, but we do not understate the difficult task of a jury in making a decision and the difficult task of a judge in summing up the case to them.

Having said that, we are quite unpersuaded that to proceed with a trial as to whether this particular consignment is proved to be household waste is an abuse of the process of the court. The judge will have regard to the 2006 Regulation and the 2007 Regulations when giving his directions to the jury. We would contemplate his raising the possibility of a breach being so small as to be minimal and not preventing waste from ceasing to be household waste and becoming waste paper under B3020. That will depend on the circumstances, including the nature and the quality, of the contamination and the amount of it. We are confident that a judge will be able to give sufficient directions to a jury to enable them to make the decision as to whether a particular consignment is properly described as household waste and for them to perform their task by applying that test to the facts."

R v KV[49]

"Assuming that this is an offence involving strict liability, it does not, in our judgment, fail for disproportionality for that reason. Sentence in a court in England or Wales is at large and discretionary; there is ample power in the court to avoid imprisonment, or indeed serious punishment, if a defendant has genuinely offended entirely without fault. The theoretical possibility of a transporter of waste being duped into transporting it without any means of knowing he is doing so would exist also if the offence were limited in the way contended for by the defendants to physical crossing of the last Member State

[49] [2012] Env. L.R. 15

boundary. For both environmental and public health reasons, the handling of waste is very closely managed under EU Regulation 1013/2006 and the international instruments to which we have referred, the Basel Convention and the OECD decision. That involves imposing considerable duties of supervision and enquiry on those who handle such material. Regulation 23 catches anyone breaching article 36(1), anyone involved in a prohibited export. That is a wider category than notifier, which is just one of the categories falling within regulation 5, where transport and person who transports are defined. As we have found, when regulation 23 prohibits transport of waste in breach of article 36(1), it states what article 36(1) intended. The UK regulations do not widen the scope of article 36(1) but merely give effect to it when read in conjunction with the definitions in article 2 of the EU Regulation. We are not persuaded by the defendants' arguments that regulation 23, coupled with regulation 5, is disproportionate."

R v Ezeemo (Godwin Chukwnaenya)[50]

"71. The scheme of the UK 2007 Regulations is to create a series of offences comprising breaches of the requirements of the EC 2006 Regulation. For example, reg.17 provides that "a person commits an offence if he fails to comply with art.49(1)" (which requires management of shipments of shipments of waste in an environmentally sound manner and without endangering human health). Articles 19 and 20 penalise a person who transports waste without meeting procedural requirements of the EC 2006 Regulation. Article 21 provides that a person commits an offence if he transports waste destined for disposal in a third country in breach of art.34 (which prohibits certain exports). Article 22 creates an offence if a person who transports waste fails to comply with art.35 procedural requirements or destinations. Article 24 creates an offence if a person transports waste without complying with the procedural requirements of art.38. Similar offences are created by regs 25–

[50] [2013] 4 All E.R. 1016; [2013] Env. L.R. 15

35 for breaches of arts 40–48. Regulations 37–39 provide that an operator of a facility commits an offence if he fails to meet certain procedural requirements of arts 10, 15, 16, 18, 20 and 22. Parallel offences are created in respect of consignees, laboratory operators, notifiers and persons who arrange the shipment of waste.

72. All of these offences use the language of close regulation in pursuit of the safe management and shipment of waste. The offences are created for failure to take the procedural steps required by the EC 2006 Regulation or the taking of a step which is prohibited by the Regulation. In our judgment, this is the language of strict liability."

R v Biffa Waste Services Limited[51]

"42. We think it important to emphasise at the outset that Article 36 of the 2006 Regulation, and therefore regulation 23 of the 2007 Regulations, are concerned with the prohibition of exports of certain wastes destined for recovery in non-OECD Decision countries. Consistently with the aims of the Basel Convention, which as we have noted at [2] reflects the need for measures relating to the transboundary movement and disposal of wastes "whatever the place of disposal", no distinction is drawn between individual non-OECD Decision countries. The Regulation thus prohibits the export of the proscribed wastes to any non-OECD Decision country, regardless of the precise destination.

43. It follows, as both parties recognise, that the correct categorisation of the waste material in question must be determined as at the point where its export begins: here, when the loaded containers left the Edmonton facility. If at that stage the material is properly categorised as Y46 household waste, its export to a non-OECD Decision country is unlawful, regardless of what might happen to it when it reaches its destination.

[51] [2020] EWCA Crim 827

> 44. Where, as in this case, waste has been collected as mixed recyclable household waste, it (or some of it) can only become paper by being properly sorted. In this context, "properly sorted" means that the sorting is sufficient to remove contaminants to the point where any contamination which remains is "so small as to be minimal and not preventing waste from becoming waste paper under B3020" (see *Ideal Waste* at [44]). If that minimal level of contamination has not been achieved by the time the export to a non-OECD Decision country begins, the material remains Y46 household waste: the prohibition therefore applies, even if further sorting or processing in the country of destination would remove all but a minimal level of contaminants."

Waste ships

Recital 35 of 1013/2006 reads:

> (35) It is necessary to ensure the safe and environmentally sound management of ship dismantling in order to protect human health and the environment. Furthermore, it should be noted that a ship may become waste as defined in Article 2 of the Basel Convention and that at the same time it may be defined as a ship under other international rules. It is important to recall that work is ongoing, involving interagency cooperation between International Labour Organisation (ILO), International Maritime Organisation (IMO) and the Secretariat of the Basel Convention, to establish mandatory requirements at the global level ensuring an efficient and effective solution to the problem of ship dismantling.

Accordingly, ships that are destined to be broken up can fall within the definition of waste and, due to the fact that such ships contain hazardous components, will fall within the category of hazardous waste and are subject to the prohibition found in Article 36.

Consequently, the export of waste ships from the EU to a non-OECD country amounts to a criminal offence.

In March 2018, the Rotterdam District Court in the Netherlands sentenced Groningen-based owner Seatrade for illegal exports of vessels sent for scrapping on beaches of South Asia as this breached the EU Waste Shipment Regulation 1013/2006. Significant fines were imposed on the company and the Directors narrowly avoided prison sentences as this was the first time that such criminal charges had been pressed.

Regulation 1257/2013: The European Ship Recycling Regulation

From 31 December 2018, large commercial seagoing vessels flying the flag of an EU Member State may only be recycled in safe and sound recycling facilities included in the European list of ship recycling facilities. EU flagged ships caught by the Ship Recycling Regulation are excluded from the scope of the Waste Shipment Regulation (EC) 1013/2006.

CHAPTER NINE
ENFORCEMENT NOTICES

S.59 Environmental Protection Act 1990

59.— Powers to require removal of waste unlawfully deposited.

(1) If any controlled waste or extractive waste is deposited in or on any land in the area of a waste regulation authority or waste collection authority in contravention of section 33(1) above or regulation 12 of the Environmental Permitting Regulations, the authority may, by notice served on him, require the occupier to do either or both of the following, that is—

(a) to remove the waste from the land within a specified period not less than a period of twenty-one days beginning with the service of the notice;

(b) to take within such a period specified steps with a view to eliminating or reducing the consequences of the deposit of the waste.

(2) A person on whom any requirements are imposed under subsection (1) above may, within the period of twenty-one days mentioned in that subsection, appeal against the requirement to a magistrates' court or, in Scotland, to the sheriff by way of summary application.

(3) On any appeal under subsection (2) above the court shall quash the requirement if it is satisfied that—

(a) the appellant neither deposited nor knowingly caused nor knowingly permitted the deposit of the waste; or

(b) there is a material defect in the notice;

and in any other case shall either modify the requirement or dismiss the appeal.

(4) Where a person appeals against any requirement imposed under subsection (1) above, the requirement shall be of no effect pending the determination of the appeal; and where the court modifies the requirement or dismisses the appeal it may extend the period specified in the notice.

(5) If a person on whom a requirement imposed under subsection (1) above fails, without reasonable excuse, to comply with the requirement he shall be liable, on summary conviction, to a fine not exceeding level 5 on the standard scale and to a further fine of an amount equal to one-tenth of the greater of £5,000 or level 4 on the standard scale for each day on which the failure continues after conviction of the offence and before the authority has begun to exercise its powers under subsection (6) below.

(6) Where a person on whom a requirement has been imposed under subsection (1) above by an authority fails to comply with the requirement the authority may do what that person was required to do and may recover from him any expenses reasonably incurred by the authority in doing it.

(7) If it appears to a waste regulation authority or waste collection authority that waste has been deposited in or on any land in contravention of section 33(1) above or regulation 12 of the Environmental Permitting Regulations, and that—

(a) in order to remove or prevent pollution of land, water or air or harm to human health it is necessary that the waste be forthwith removed or other steps taken to eliminate or reduce the consequences of the deposit or both; or

(b) there is no occupier of the land or the occupier cannot be found without the authority incurring unreasonable expense; or

(c) the occupier neither made nor knowingly permitted the deposit of the waste;

the authority may remove the waste from the land or take other steps to eliminate or reduce the consequences of the deposit or, as the case may require, to remove the waste and take those steps.

(8) Where an authority exercises any of the powers conferred on it by subsection (7) above it shall be entitled to recover the cost incurred by it in removing the waste or taking the steps or both and in disposing of the waste—

(a) in a case falling within subsection (7)(a) above, from the occupier of the land unless he proves that he neither made nor knowingly caused nor knowingly permitted the deposit of the waste;

(b) in any case, from any person who deposited or knowingly caused or knowingly permitted the deposit of any of the waste;

except such of the cost as the occupier or that person shows was incurred unnecessarily.

(8A) An authority may not recover costs under subsection (8) above if a compensation order has been made under section 130 of the Powers of Criminal Courts (Sentencing) Act 2000 in favour of the authority in respect of any part of those costs.

(8B) Subsection (8A) does not apply if the order is set aside on appeal.

(9) Any waste removed by an authority under subsection (7) above shall belong to that authority and may be dealt with accordingly.

In force: 12 March 2015

S.59ZA Environmental Protection Act 1990

59ZA Section 59: supplementary power in relation to owner of land

(1) Where the grounds in subsection (2), (3) or (4) below are met, a waste regulation authority or waste collection authority may, by notice served on him, require the owner of any land in its area to comply with either or both of the requirements mentioned in subsection (1)(a) and (b) of section 59 above.

(2) The grounds in this subsection are that it appears to the authority that waste has been deposited in or on the land in contravention of section 33(1) above [or regulation 12 of the [the Environmental Permitting Regulations]3 ,]2 and–

(a) there is no occupier of the land, or

(b) the occupier cannot be found without the authority incurring unreasonable expense.

(3) The grounds in this subsection are that–

(a) the authority has served a notice under subsection (1) of section 59 above imposing a requirement on the occupier of the land,

(b) the occupier of the land is not the same person as the owner of the land, and

(c) the occupier has failed to comply with the requirement mentioned in paragraph (a) above within the period specified in the notice.

(4) The grounds in this subsection are that–

(a) the authority has served a notice under subsection (1) of section 59 above imposing a requirement on the occupier of the land,

(b) the occupier of the land is not the same person as the owner of the land, and

(c) the requirement mentioned in paragraph (a) above has been quashed on the ground specified in subsection (3)(a) of that section.

(5) Subsections (2) to (6) of section 59 above apply in relation to requirements imposed under this section on the owner of the land as they apply in relation to requirements imposed under that section on the occupier of the land but as if in subsection (3) there were inserted after paragraph (a)– "(aa) in order to comply with the requirement the appellant would be required to enter the land unlawfully; or".

(6) In this section *"owner"* has the meaning given to it in section 78A(9) below.

In force: 6 April 2010

S.59ZB Environmental Protection Act 1990

59ZB.— Powers to require removal of waste unlawfully kept or disposed of: England and Wales

(1) Subsection (2) applies if any controlled waste or extractive waste is kept or disposed of in or on any land in the area of an

authority in contravention of section 33(1) or regulation 12 of the Environmental Permitting Regulations.

(2) The authority may, by notice served on the occupier, require the occupier to do one or both of the following—
(a) remove the waste from the land within a specified period of not less than 21 days beginning with the service of the notice;
(b) take within such a period specified steps with a view to eliminating or reducing the consequences of the keeping or disposal of the waste.

(3) A person on whom a requirement is imposed under subsection (2) may, within 21 days beginning with the service of the notice, appeal against the requirement to a magistrates' court.

(4) On any appeal under subsection (3), the court must quash the requirement if it is satisfied that—

(a) the appellant did not keep or dispose of, or knowingly cause or knowingly permit the keeping or disposal of, the waste, or

(b) there is a material defect in the notice,
and in any other case may modify the requirement or dismiss the appeal.

(5) Where a person appeals against a requirement imposed under subsection (2), the requirement has no effect pending the determination of the appeal; and where the court modifies the requirement or dismisses the appeal it may extend the period specified in the notice.

(6) If a person on whom a requirement imposed under subsection (2) fails, without reasonable excuse, to comply with the requirement, that person is liable, on summary conviction, to a fine.

(7) Where a person on whom a requirement has been imposed under subsection (2) by an authority fails to comply with the

requirement, the authority may do what that person was required to do and may recover from that person any expenses reasonably incurred by the authority in doing it.

(8) If it appears to an authority that controlled waste or extractive waste has been kept or disposed of in or on any land in the authority's area in contravention of section 33(1) or regulation 12 of the Environmental Permitting Regulations, and that—

(a) in order to remove or prevent pollution of land, water or air or harm to human health, it is necessary that the waste be forthwith removed, or that steps are taken to eliminate or reduce the consequences of the keeping or disposal, or both,

(b) there is no occupier of the land or the occupier cannot be found without the authority incurring unreasonable expense, or

(c) the occupier did not keep or dispose of, or knowingly cause or knowingly permit the keeping or disposal of, the waste,

the authority may remove the waste from the land, or take steps to eliminate or reduce the consequences of the keeping or disposal of the waste, or both.

(9) Where an authority exercises any of the powers conferred on it by subsection (8), it is entitled to recover the cost incurred by it in removing the waste or taking the steps or both, and in disposing of the waste—

(a) in a case falling within subsection (8)(a), from the occupier of the land, unless the occupier proves that the occupier did not keep or dispose of, or knowingly cause or knowingly permit the keeping or disposal of, the waste,

(b) in any case, from any person who kept or disposed of, or knowingly caused or knowingly permitted the keeping or disposal of, the waste, except such of the cost as the occupier or that person shows was incurred unnecessarily.

(10) An authority may not recover costs under subsection (9) if a compensation order has been made under section 130 of the Powers of Criminal Courts (Sentencing) Act 20002 in favour of the authority in respect of any part of those costs.

(11) Subsection (10) does not apply if the compensation order is set aside on appeal.

(12) Any waste removed by an authority under subsection (8) belongs to that authority and may be dealt with accordingly.

(13) Subsections (2) and (8) do not apply in relation to household waste from a domestic property which is kept or disposed of within the curtilage of that property by a person other than an establishment or undertaking.

(14) In this section and section 59ZC, *"authority"* means—
(a) a waste regulation authority in England or Wales, or
(b) a waste collection authority in England or Wales.

In force: 8 May 2018

S.59ZC Environmental Protection Act 1990

59ZC.— Section 59ZB: supplementary power in relation to owner of land

(1) Where the grounds in subsection (2) or (3) are met, an authority may, by notice served on the owner of any land in its area, require the owner to comply with one or both of the requirements mentioned in section 59ZB(2)(a) or (b).

(2) The grounds in this subsection are that it appears to the authority that controlled waste or extractive waste has been

kept or disposed of in or on the land in contravention of section 33(1) or regulation 12 of the Environmental Permitting Regulations, and—

(a) there is no occupier of the land, or

(b) the occupier cannot be found without the authority incurring unreasonable expense.

(3) The grounds in this subsection are that—

(a) the authority has served a notice under section 59ZB(2) imposing a requirement on the occupier of the land,

(b) the occupier of the land is not the same person as the owner of the land, and

(c) either—

(i) the occupier has failed to comply with the requirement mentioned in paragraph (a) within the period specified in the notice, or

(ii) the requirement mentioned in paragraph (a) has been quashed on the ground specified in section 59ZB(4)(a).

(4) Section 59ZB(3) to (7) apply in relation to a requirement imposed under this section on the owner of the land as they apply in relation to a requirement imposed under that section on the occupier of land but as if in section 59ZB(4) there were inserted after paragraph (a)—

(aa) in order to comply with the requirement the appellant would be required to enter the land unlawfully, or".

(5) Subsection (1) does not apply in relation to household waste from a domestic property which is kept or disposed of

within the curtilage of that property by a person other than an establishment or undertaking.

(6) In this section, *"owner"* has the meaning given by section 78A(9)

In force: 8 May 2018

Neal Soil Suppliers Ltd v Environment Agency[52]

> "23. I have set out the terms of s.59(1) earlier, but what is obvious is that that latter provision not only empowers the service of a notice to require both removal of the waste and specified steps to eliminate or reduce the consequences of the deposit; a notice can also require either of those two things; that is to say, it can require merely removal of the waste, or it can require merely the taking of "specified steps" under s.59(1)(b) . In other words, a s.59 notice may perfectly lawfully allow the waste to remain deposited on the land in question, albeit that the deposit breached s.33 and the notice may simply require some steps short of removal to be taken.
>
> 24. It is self-evident that this last course of action must normally involve allowing the occupier to "keep" the waste on his land, even though that in itself would otherwise be an offence under s.31(1)(b). Likewise, it must be the case that the notice under s.59 can require the occupier to "treat" the waste in some way. "Treat", it should be noted, has a wide meaning under the 1990 Act: see s.29(6). Consequently, s.33(1) must be read subject to the provisions of s.59(1). Action taken in compliance with the requirements of the s.59(1) notice will not amount to a criminal offence under s.33(1). That is entirely accepted, as I have indicated earlier, by the respondent. Insofar as the judgment of the Crown Court was based on the contrary view, as it seems to me that it was, it was erroneous."

---

[52] [2008] Env. L.R. 15

...

29. The object of s.59 is not to make good any deficiencies in the penalties imposed in the course of criminal proceedings. Those penalties can prevent a person obtaining any commercial advantage from breaching the licensing system, and they are adequate to do so. Indeed, for my part, I would encourage Magistrates' Courts before whom prosecutions are brought, or for that matter Crown Courts before which any prosecution comes on indictment, to reflect in any financial penalty imposed the amount of commercial advantage which has been obtained by a person through the unlawful deposit of controlled waste. But having said that, the task of the court on a s.59 appeal is to decide the most appropriate remedial steps in the context of protecting human health and protecting the environment. That is the approach which it should adopt. After all, in any such appeal an offence would have been committed, and if there was to be the sort of approach adopted by the Crown Court here, then in almost every case one could find the court preferring, on no other good or pragmatic grounds, the course of removal rather than treatment. No such presumption seems to me to be implied in the provisions of s.59.

Enforcement Notices

Reg 36 Environmental Permitting (England and Wales) Regulations 2016

36.— Enforcement notices

(1) If the regulator considers that an operator has contravened, is contravening, or is likely to contravene an environmental permit condition, the regulator may serve a notice on the operator.

(2) The notice must—

(a) state the regulator's view under paragraph (1),

(b) specify the matters constituting the contravention or making a contravention likely,

(c) specify the steps that must be taken to remedy the contravention or to ensure that the likely contravention does not occur, and

(d) specify the period within which those steps must be taken.

(3) Steps that may be specified in the notice include steps—

(a) to make the operation of a regulated facility comply with the environmental permit conditions, and

(b) to remedy the environmental effects caused by the contravention.

(4) In paragraph (3)(b) *"environmental effects"* means—

(a) in relation to a flood risk activity—

(i) flooding or risk of flooding;

(ii) detrimental impact on drainage or risk of detrimental impact on drainage;

(iii) harm to the environment or risk of harm to the environment;

(b) in relation to any other class of regulated facility, the effects of pollution.

(5) In the case of a regulated facility to which Schedule 7, 13 or 14 applies, if the regulator considers that an incident or accident significantly affecting the environment has occurred as

the result of the operation of that regulated facility, the regulator may serve a notice on the operator of that facility.

(6) A notice served under paragraph (5) must—

(a) specify the measures necessary to limit the environmental consequences of the incident or accident, and

(b) specify the measures necessary to prevent further incidents or accidents.

(7) The regulator may withdraw a notice under this regulation at any time by further notice served on the operator.

General observations

Enforcement notices are, at least in theory, a cost-effective way for the Environment Agency to address non-compliances within permitted facilities.

Appeals against an enforcement notice are made to the Planning Inspectorate. Guidance for an appeal was last updated in March 2019[53]. This includes guidance on the various time limits and procedures. Appeals do not suspend the effect of the notice. In certain circumstances, consideration should be given to judicially reviewing the notice at the same time as launching an appeal, with a view to applying for interim relief preventing the operation of the notice.

---

[53] https://assets.publishing.service.gov.uk/government/uploads/system/uploads/attachment_data/file/831106/EP_appeal_guide_September_2019.pdf, last accessed 3 November 2020

Suspension Notices

Reg 37 Environmental Permitting (England and Wales) Regulations 2016

37.— Suspension notices

(1) The regulator may suspend an environmental permit by serving a notice (a "suspension notice") on the operator under this regulation.

(2) If the regulator considers that the operation of a regulated facility under an environmental permit involves a risk of serious pollution or, in the case of a flood risk activity, a risk specified in paragraph (3), it may serve a suspension notice on the operator.

(3) The following are risks specified for the purposes of paragraph (2)—

(a) risk of serious flooding;

(b) risk of serious detrimental impact on drainage;

(c) risk of serious harm to the environment.

(4) Paragraph (2) applies whether or not the manner of operating the regulated facility which involves the risk is subject to or contravenes an environmental permit condition.

(5) If the regulator considers that the manner of operating a regulated facility contravenes an environmental permit condition, and that such contravention involves a risk of pollution or, in the case of a flood risk activity, a risk specified in paragraph (6), it may serve a suspension notice on the operator.

(6) The following are risks specified for the purposes of paragraph (5)—

(a) risk of flooding;

(b) risk of detrimental impact on drainage;

(c) risk of harm to the environment.

(7) A suspension notice served for the purpose of paragraph (2) or (5) must—

(a) specify—

(i) the risk mentioned in paragraph (2) or (5),

(ii) the steps that must be taken to remove that risk,

(iii) in a case where paragraph (5) applies, the matters constituting the contravention mentioned in that paragraph,

(iv) in a case where paragraph (5) applies, the steps that must be taken to remedy that contravention, and

(v) the period within which the steps mentioned in paragraph (ii) or (iv) must be taken,

(b) state that the environmental permit ceases to have effect to the extent specified in the notice until the notice is withdrawn, and

(c) if the environmental permit continues to authorise the operation of a regulated facility, state any steps (in addition to those already required to be taken by the environmental permit conditions) that are to be taken when operating that regulated facility.

(8) The regulator may suspend an environmental permit under regulation 66(5) by serving a suspension notice on the operator.

(9) A suspension notice served for the purpose of paragraph (8) must—

(a) specify the reason for the suspension,

(b) state the sum payable by the operator and the period within which it is to be paid, and

(c) state that the environmental permit ceases to have effect to the extent specified in the notice until the notice is withdrawn.

(10) If a suspension notice is served, the environmental permit ceases to have effect to the extent stated in the notice.

(11) Where a suspension notice has the effect of preventing waste of a specified description being accepted at a regulated facility, the notice may require the operator of that facility to display appropriate signs at such places as may be specified in the notice, informing the public that no further waste of a specified description may be accepted at that facility.

(12) The regulator—

(a) may withdraw a suspension notice at any time by further notice served on the operator, and

(b) must withdraw a notice when satisfied that the steps specified in it have been taken.

General observations

The assessment of whether or not a risk of serious pollution exists is a matter for the Environment Agency, essentially challengeable in public law only on grounds of irrationality.

Subsection (7) imposes a mandatory obligation on the Environment Agency to specify the steps that must be taken. This cannot be satisfied by a general requirement to implement measures to meet an identified risk.

As with enforcement notices, appeals are made to the Planning Inspectorate. Appeals do not suspend the effect of the notice. In certain circumstances, consideration should be given to judicially reviewing the notice at the same time as launching an appeal, with a view to applying for an interim relief preventing the operation of the notice.

Key cases

R (on the application of European Metal Recycling Ltd) v Environment Agency[54]:

> "18. The question whether there is such a risk is manifestly one for the judgment of the EA. Such a judgment is capable of challenge only on irrationality grounds. In my view such a challenge is clearly unarguable on the facts of this case. All the material available to the EA has to be viewed in the round when considering this issue. The material referred to in the internal decision making record so considered clearly entitled the EA to conclude that a risk of serious pollution was made out and clearly made out."
>
> ...
>
> "24. Schedule 2 to the [suspension notice] specifies the steps that have to be taken as being to, "... design and implement measures that eliminate the risk of serious pollution from noise". As a matter of language a requirement to state explicitly the steps required to be taken to eliminate an identified risk cannot sensibly be said to be satisfied by a requirement to design and implement measures to eliminate that risk. There is no material difference between a measure and a step, or between "eliminate" and "remove", or between "taken" and

[54] [2013] Env. L.R. 14

"design and implement" in this context. In my judgment it is obvious as a matter of language that a requirement to state explicitly the steps that must be taken to remove an identified risk is not satisfied by a statement requiring the recipient to take steps to remove the identified risk. If this is correct as a matter of language I do not see how a requirement to design and implement measures to eliminate the risk is any more compliant. Had the EA's position been that any noise emanating from the Site as a result of regulated activity pursuant to the Permit had to be eliminated then it might have been possible to say that a provision to this effect was satisfactory because it required the elimination of all noise. However, it is not the EA's case that this is what is required. Thus it seems to me that as a matter of language, what is required for Sch.2 to be compliant with reg.37(4)(a)(ii) is the identification of either outcomes or criteria that have to be achieved by whatever means EMR choose to adopt and/or the identification of specific steps that are required to be taken."

…

"34. Where the effect of a statutory appeal is that the [suspension notice] is not suspended pending determination of the appeal, and where, as here, the effect of such a notice is to require all regulated activity governed by the relevant permit to be discontinued and where, as here, it is likely that an appeal will take months rather than weeks to be determined, in my judgment it is difficult to conclude that the existence of a statutory appeal is either equally effective or convenient. The losses caused to EMR by a suspension in the terms adopted by the EA in this case would inevitably be substantial and the potential effect on employees at the Site even more serious. In addition there is a fundamental issue of law that requires resolution—that is the degree to which if at all EPR 10 requires the specification of the steps required to be taken. It was clearly desirable that a ruling on this issue be obtained in early course. A statutory appeal is not the most appropriate method for deciding such issues—see *R v. Falmouth and Truro PHA v South West Water Ltd* (ante) at 473D-F."

S.109A-N Environment Act 1995

Sections 109A-N provide the Environment Agency (and Natural Resources Wales) with the power to issue restriction notices and apply for a "restriction order".

The regulator can prohibit access to and the importation of waste into, a site where there is, or was, a regulated facility or an exempt facility (or a part of it) for a specified period, in circumstances where:

(i) there is a risk of serious pollution to the environment or serious harm to human health at the site as a result of the treatment, keeping, deposit or disposal of waste; and

(ii) intervention is required to prevent the risk from continuing.

To take such action, the regulator must issue a "restriction notice", which is effective for up to 72 hours or apply to the court for a "restriction order", which can have effect for up to 6 months and can be extended, varied or discharged. Prior to issuing a restriction notice, the regulator is required to make reasonable efforts to inform the occupier (or owner) that the notice will be issued and to consult with them on the arrangements for any access, which is required to the premises for purposes such as maintaining machinery or securing the site. The restriction notice will not prevent the occupier or owner itself from accessing the waste site.

To date, the use of a restriction order has been reasonably limited and the authors are not aware of any appeals against the imposition of a restriction order. This in itself may not be surprising, given the fact that the power is a relatively recent one.

CHAPTER TEN
SENTENCING

Sentencing will take place either after the defendant has been convicted following a trial or where the defendant has pleaded guilty. Sentencing procedure is similar in the Magistrates Court and Crown Court.

Where a defendant pleads guilty, ordinarily in environmental cases a defendant will submit a basis of plea, setting out the basis on which the plea is entered and identifying what part of the prosecution case is accepted and what part is not. If this is not accepted by the prosecution and/or the Court and the tribunal is of the view that there would be a material difference to the level of sentence, then there may be a Newton hearing. At a Newton hearing, the tribunal will determine the factual basis on which sentencing will take place.

The dangers of not specifying the basis on which a guilty plea is tendered was set out in *R v Friskies Petcare Ltd* [2000] 2 Cr.App.R. (S.) 401 in the context of Health and Safety prosecutions. Subsequent judicial guidance has also stated the importance of clearly setting out the basis of any plea, particularly in areas of law that are not so familiar to the criminal courts. Further, it is good practice for the prosecution to set out clearly a summary of the offence and where culpability and harm lay before any plea is entered.

Environmental Offences Definitive Guideline

Any organisation or individual sentenced for relevant offences after 1st July 2014, no matter when they were committed, falls to be dealt with according to the Environmental Offences Definitive Guidelines. The guidelines apply to the following offences: Unauthorised or harmful deposit, treatment or disposal etc of waste/ Illegal discharges to air, land and water, Environmental Permitting (England and Wales) Regulations

2010, regulations 12 and 38(1), (2) and (3) and the Environmental Protection Act 1990, s.33.

There are other relevant and analogous environmental offences to which these guidelines apply but the user must take into account any differences in maximum sentence between these and the ones listed above. The court should refer to the sentencing approach in steps one to three and five and six of the guidelines, adjusting the starting points and ranges bearing in mind the statutory maxima for those offences. These offences are:

Section 1 Control of Pollution (Amendment) Act 1989 – transporting controlled waste without registering;

Section 34 Environmental Protection Act 1990 – breach of duty of care. Section 80 Environmental Protection Act 1990 – breach of an abatement notice;

Section 111 Water Industry Act 1991 – restrictions on use of public sewers;

Offences under the Transfrontier Shipment of Waste Regulations 2007.

Section 125(1) of the Coroners and Justice Act 2009 provides that when sentencing offences committed after 6 April 2010:

> "Every court –
>
> must, in sentencing an offender, follow any sentencing guideline which is relevant to the offender's case, and
>
> must, in exercising any other function relating to the sentencing of offenders, follow any sentencing guidelines which are relevant to the exercise of the function,
>
> unless the court is satisfied that it would be contrary to the interests of justice to do so."

Structure, ranges and starting points

The guideline specifies the range of sentences appropriate for each type of offence. Within each offence, there are a number of categories which reflect varying degrees of seriousness. The offence range is split into category ranges. There is a starting point within each category. Starting points define the position within a category range from which to start calculating the sentence. The court should consider in a chronological stepped process, further features of the offence or the offender that warrant adjustment of the sentence within the range. Starting points and ranges apply to all offenders, whether they have pleaded guilty or been convicted after trial. Credit for a guilty plea is taken into consideration only at step nine after the appropriate sentence has been identified. The maximum sentence that applies to an offence is the maximum that applied at the date of the offence.

Sentencing should reflect the defendant's ability to pay. Fines should be significant enough to bring home the seriousness of the offending to corporate organisations and so identifying a company's turnover is an important stage. Corporate defendants are required to produce accounts and in practice this means the last three full sets of accounts filed. However, if an organisation's profit relative to its turnover is small a downward adjustment to the fine may be made.

Sentencing Organisations

Step 1 – Compensation

The court must consider making a compensation order requiring the offender to pay compensation for any personal injury, loss or damage resulting from the offence in such an amount as the court considers appropriate, having regard to the evidence and to the means of the offender. Where the means of the offender are limited, priority should be given to the payment of compensation over payment of any other financial penalty. Reasons should be given if a compensation order is not made.

(See section 130 Powers of Criminal Courts (Sentencing) Act 2000)

Step 2 – Confiscation (Crown Court only)

Confiscation must be considered if either the Crown asks for it or the court thinks that it may be appropriate. Confiscation must be dealt with before any other fine or financial order (except compensation).
(See sections 6 and 13 Proceeds of Crime Act 2002)

Step 3 – Determining the offence category

The court should determine the offence category using only the culpability and harm factors set out in the Guideline. The culpability and harm categories are on a sliding scale; there is inevitable overlap between the factors described in adjacent categories. Where an offence does not fall squarely into a category, individual factors may require a degree of weighting before making an overall assessment and determining the appropriate offence category.

Dealing with a risk of harm involves consideration of both the likelihood of harm occurring and the extent of it if it does. Risk of harm is less serious than the same actual harm. Where the offence has caused risk of harm but no (or less) actual harm the normal approach is to move down to the next category of harm. This may not be appropriate if either the likelihood or extent of potential harm is particularly high.

Culpability

Deliberate

Intentional breach of or flagrant disregard for the law by person(s) whose position of responsibility in the organisation is such that their acts/omissions can properly be attributed to the organisation;

OR

deliberate failure by organisation to put in place and to enforce such systems as could reasonably be expected in all the circumstances to avoid commission of the offence.

Reckless

Actual foresight of, or wilful blindness to, risk of offending but risk nevertheless taken by person(s) whose position of responsibility in the organisation is such that their acts/ omissions can properly be attributed to the organisation;

OR

reckless failure by organisation to put in place and to enforce such systems as could reasonably be expected in all the circumstances to avoid commission of the offence.

Negligent

Failure by the organisation as a whole to take reasonable care to put in place and enforce proper systems for avoiding commission of the offence.

Low or no culpability

Offence committed with little or no fault on the part of the organisation as a whole, for example by accident or the act of a rogue employee and despite the presence and due enforcement of all reasonably required preventive measures, or where such proper preventive measures were unforeseeably overcome by exceptional events.

Harm

Category 1

- Polluting material of a dangerous nature, for example, hazardous chemicals or sharp objects;
- Major adverse effect or damage to air or water quality, amenity value, or property;
- Polluting material was noxious, widespread or pervasive with long lasting effects on human health or quality of life, animal health or flora;

- Major costs incurred through clean-up, site restoration or animal rehabilitation;
- Major interference with, prevention or undermining of other lawful activities or regulatory regime due to offence

Category 2

- Significant adverse effect or damage to air or water quality, amenity value, or property;
- Significant adverse effect on human health or quality of life, animal health or flora;
- Significant costs incurred through clean-up, site restoration or animal rehabilitation;
- Significant interference with or undermining of other lawful activities or regulatory regime due to offence;
- Risk of category 1 harm.

Category 3

- Minor, localised adverse effect or damage to air or water quality, amenity value, or property;
- Minor adverse effect on human health or quality of life, animal health or flora;
- Low costs incurred through clean-up, site restoration or animal rehabilitation;
- Limited interference with or undermining of other lawful activities or regulatory regime due to offence;
- Risk of category 2 harm.

Category 4

- Risk of category 3 harm

Step 4 – Starting point and category range

Having determined the category, the court should refer to the tables in the Guideline. There are four tables of starting points and ranges: one for large organisations, one for medium organisations, one for small organisations and one for micro-organisations. The court should refer to the table that relates to the size of the offending organisation and should use the corresponding starting point to reach a sentence within the category range. The court should then consider further adjustment within the category range for aggravating and mitigating features.

In *R v Lawrence* [2020] EWCA Crim 1465, the Court of Appeal took the opportunity to reiterate that the Definitive Guideline for sentencing environmental offences is not a statute and can, where cases merit it, afford a great deal of flexibility to the sentencing Judge. In this case, the appellant was the operations director and technically competent person of a waste business that suffered multiple waste fires. He had pleaded guilty to four offences, two in relation to the first fire in December 2012 and two in relation to the second fire in June 2013. The Judge at the sentencing hearing that the cumulative effect of the category 2 features had the potential to raise the overall harm into category 1 and that there were multiple aggravating features. The sentence imposed was 9 months imprisonment, suspended for 2 years and 180 hours of unpaid work.

The Court of Appeal found that there were ample findings made by the Judge to justify finding harm at the top of category 2 with other features available in the offending to aggravate the offending well beyond that. The Guideline explicitly states that "*in some cases, having considered these [aggravating] factors, it may be appropriate to move outside the category range*".

General principles to follow in setting a fine

The fine must reflect the seriousness of the offence and the court to take into account the financial circumstances of the offender, section 164 of the Criminal Justice Act 2003. The level of fine should reflect the extent to which the offender fell below the required standard. The fine should meet, in a fair and proportionate way, the objectives of punishment, deterrence and the removal of gain derived through the commission of the offence; it should not be cheaper to offend than to take the appropriate precautions. Fines for organisations are based primarily on turnover although there is a stage at which the court can consider the net profit relative to the turnover and make any appropriate adjustment.

The coming into force of the Guideline has seen an increase in the levels of fines imposed on corporate defendants.

Obtaining financial information

Offenders which are companies, partnerships or bodies delivering a public or charitable service, are expected to provide comprehensive accounts for the last three years, to enable the court to make an accurate assessment of its financial status. In the absence of such disclosure, or where the court is not satisfied that it has been given sufficient reliable information, the court will be entitled to draw reasonable inferences as to the offender's means from evidence it has heard and from all the circumstances of the case.

Normally, only information relating to the organisation before the court will be relevant, unless it is demonstrated to the court that the resources of a linked organisation are available and can properly be taken into account.

For companies, the court will examine the annual accounts. Particular attention should be paid to turnover; profit before tax; directors' remuneration, loan accounts and pension provision and assets as disclosed by the balance sheet. Most companies are required to file audited accounts at Companies House.

For partnerships' annual accounts particular attention should be paid to turnover; profit before tax; partners' drawings, loan accounts and pension provision; assets as above. Limited Liability Partnerships (LLPs) may be required to file audited accounts with Companies House.

For local authorities, fire authorities and similar public bodies the Annual Revenue Budget ("ARB") is the equivalent of turnover and the best indication of the size of the defendant organisation. It is unlikely to be necessary to analyse specific expenditure or reserves (where relevant) unless inappropriate expenditure is suggested.

For health trusts: the independent regulator of NHS Foundation Trusts is Monitor. It publishes quarterly reports and annual figures for the financial strength and stability of trusts from which the annual income can be seen, available via www.monitor-nhsft.gov.uk. Detailed analysis of expenditure or reserves is unlikely to be called for.

For charities: it will be appropriate to inspect annual audited accounts. Detailed analysis of expenditure or reserves is unlikely to be called for unless there is a suggestion of unusual or unnecessary expenditure. Where the fine will fall on public or charitable bodies, the fine should normally be substantially reduced if the offending organisation is able to demonstrate the proposed fine would have a significant impact on the provision of their services. However, substantially reduced does not mean more than 50% and the amount of reduction will be a matter for the court, *R v University College London [2018] EWCA 835 (Crim),*

At step four, the court will be required to focus on the organisation's annual turnover or equivalent to reach a starting point for a fine. At step six, the court may be required to refer to the other financial factors listed above to ensure that the proposed fine is proportionate.

Very large organisations

Where a defendant company's turnover or equivalent very greatly exceeds the threshold for large companies, it may be necessary to move outside the suggested range to achieve a proportionate sentence. This is not defined in the Guideline and the Courts have consistently declined to provide any form of mathematical formula. Each case will turn on its own facts.

However, it is important to note that the power to move outside of the suggested range is a discretionary one and will not be applied in each and every case involving a very large organisation. For example, if a very large organisation can demonstrate a high degree of responsibility and a commitment to the environment, it may be considered that such a move is unnecessary.

In *R v Thames Water Utilities Ltd [2015] EWCA Crim 960*, the Court of Appeal gave important guidance on imposing fines for environmental offences on organisations that are significantly larger than the "large companies" covered by the Guideline. The court placed particular emphasis on fines being high enough to send a strong message to company directors and shareholders about their environmental obligations.

In 2017, Thames Water Utilities Ltd received a fine of £20 million for a series of pollution incidents following guilty pleas to a number of offences contrary to the Environmental Permitting (England and Wales) Regulations 2010.

In a further case involving Thames Water in 2019, in *R v Thames Water Utilities Ltd [2019] EWCA Crim 1344 (26 July 2019)*, the Court of Appeal approved its 2015 case guidance which it considered provided more than satisfactory guidance on the approach to be taken by judges.

Large - Turnover or equivalent: £50 million and over

Large	Starting Point	Range
Deliberate		
Category 1	£1,000,000	£450,000 – £3,000,000
Category 2	£500,000	£180,000 – £1,250,000
Category 3	£180,000	£100,000 – £450,000
Category 4	£100,000	£55,000 – £250,000
Reckless		
Category 1	£550,000	£250,000 – £1,500,000
Category 2	£250,000	£100,000 – £650,000
Category 3	£100,000	£60,000 – £250,000
Category 4	£60,000	£35,000 – £160,000
Negligent		
Category 1	£300,000	£140,000 – £750,000
Category 2	£140,000	£60,000 – £350,000
Category 3	£60,000	£35,000 – £150,000
Category 4	£35,000	£22,000 – £100,000
Low / No culpability		
Category 1	£50,000	£25,000 – £130,000
Category 2	£25,000	£14,000 – £70,000
Category 3	£14,000	£10,000 – £40,000
Category 4	£10,000	£7,000 - £25,000

Medium - Turnover or equivalent: between £10 million and £50 million

Medium	Starting Point	Range
Deliberate		
Category 1	£400,000	£170,000 – £1,000,000
Category 2	£170,000	£70,000 – £450,000
Category 3	£70,000	£40,000 – £180,000
Category 4	£40,000	£22,000 – £100,000
Reckless		
Category 1	£220,000	£100,000 – £500,000
Category 2	£100,000	£40,000 – £250,000
Category 3	£40,000	£24,000 – £100,000
Category 4	£24,000	£14,000 – £60,000
Negligent		
Category 1	£120,000	£55,000 – £300,000
Category 2	£55,000	£25,000 – £140,000
Category 3	£25,000	£14,000 – £60,000
Category 4	£14,000	£8,000 – £35,000
Low / No culpability		
Category 1	£20,000	£10,000 – £50,000
Category 2	£10,000	£5,500 – £25,000
Category 3	£5,000	£3,500 – £14,000
Category 4	£3,000	£2,500 – £10,000

Small - Turnover or equivalent: between £2 million and £10 million

Small	Starting Point	Range
Deliberate		
Category 1	£100,000	£45,000 – £400,000
Category 2	£45,000	£17,000 – £170,000
Category 3	£17,000	£10,000 – £70,000
Category 4	£10,000	£5,000 – £40,000
Reckless		
Category 1	£55,000	£24,000 – £220,000
Category 2	£24,000	£10,000 – £100,000
Category 3	£10,000	£5,000 – £40,000
Category 4	£5,000	£3,000 – £24,000
Negligent		
Category 1	£30,000	£13,000 – £120,000
Category 2	£13,000	£6,000 – £55,000
Category 3	£6,000	£3,000 – £23,000
Category 4	£3,000	£1,500 – £14,000
Low / No culpability		
Category 1	£5,000	£2,500 – £20,000
Category 2	£2,500	£1,000 – £10,000
Category 3	£1,000	£700 – £5,000
Category 4	£700	£400 – £3,500

Micro - Turnover or equivalent: not more than £2 million

Micro	Starting Point	Range
Deliberate		
Category 1	£50,000	£9,000 – £95,000
Category 2	£22,000	£3,000 – £45,000
Category 3	£9,000	£2,000 – £17,000
Category 4	£5,000	£1,000 – £10,000
Reckless		
Category 1	£30,000	£3,000 – £55,000
Category 2	£12,000	£1,500 – £24,000
Category 3	£5,000	£1,000 – £10,000
Category 4	£3,000	£500 – £5,500
Negligent		
Category 1	£15,000	£1,500 – £30,000
Category 2	£6,500	£1,000 – £13,000
Category 3	£2,500	£500 – £5,500
Category 4	£1,400	£350 – £3,000
Low / No culpability		
Category 1	£2,500	£500 – £5,000
Category 2	£1,000	£350 – £2,400
Category 3	£400	£175 – £1,000
Category 4	£200	£100 – £700

Aggravating and mitigating features

The Guideline provides a non-exhaustive list of factual elements providing the context of the offence and factors relating to the offender. The Court is required to identify whether any combination of these, or other relevant factors, should result in an upward or downward adjustment from the starting point. In particular, relevant recent convictions and/or a history of non-compliance are likely to result in a substantial upward adjustment. In some cases, having considered these factors, it may be appropriate to move outside the identified category range.

Factors increasing seriousness

Statutory aggravating factors

Previous convictions

Care should be taken to avoid double counting factors including those already taken into account in assessing culpability or harm or those inherent in the offence.

Guidance on the use of previous convictions

The following guidance should be considered when seeking to determine the degree to which previous convictions should aggravate sentence: Section 143 of the Criminal Justice Act 2003 states that:

> "In considering the seriousness of an offence ("the current offence") committed by an offender who has one or more previous convictions, the court must treat each previous conviction as an aggravating factor if (in the case of that conviction) the court considers that it can reasonably be so treated having regard, in particular, to—
>
> (a) the nature of the offence to which the conviction relates and its relevance to the current offence, and

(b) the time that has elapsed since the conviction."

Previous convictions are considered at step two in the Council's offence-specific guidelines.

Other aggravating factors include

- History of non-compliance with warnings by regulator
- Location of the offence, for example, near housing, schools, livestock or environmentally sensitive sites
- Repeated incidents of offending or offending over an extended period of time, where not charged separately
- Deliberate concealment of illegal nature of activity
- Ignoring risks identified by employees or others
- Established evidence of wider/community impact
- Breach of any order
- Offence committed for financial gain
- Obstruction of justice

Care should be taken to avoid double counting factors including those already taken into account in assessing culpability or harm or those inherent in the offence

Where an offender has had the benefit of warnings or advice about their conduct but has failed to heed it, this would make the offender more blameworthy. This may particularly be the case when: such warning(s) or advice were of an official nature or from a professional source and/or the warning(s) were made at the time of or shortly before the commission of the offence.

Offence committed for financial gain

Where an offence (which is not one which by its nature is an acquisitive offence) has been committed wholly or in part for financial gain or the avoidance of cost, this will increase the seriousness. Where the offending is committed in a commercial context for financial gain or the avoidance of costs, this will normally indicate a higher level of culpability.

Factors reducing seriousness or reflecting mitigation

No previous convictions or no relevant/recent convictions

First time offenders are often able to argue that because the offending behaviour was out of character, it is less likely to occur again and that such a factor should warrant a lower penalty. Further, a person, including an organisation, who loses his good character, can often argue that this alone has had a significant impact on it. Such a person may be regarded as less blame-worthy and present a lower risk of re-offending. usually represent a lower risk of reoffending.

Where there are previous offences but these are old and /or are for offending of a different nature, the sentence might be reduced to reflect those factors or alternatively the previous convictions not given significant weight.

Evidence of steps taken to remedy problem

Remorse

The court will need to be satisfied that the offender is genuinely remorseful for the offending behaviour in order to reduce the sentence (separate from any guilty plea reduction). Lack of remorse should never be treated as an aggravating factor.

Compensation paid voluntarily to remedy harm caused

One-off event not commercially motivated

Little or no financial gain

Where an offence (which is not one which by its nature is an acquisitive offence) is committed in a context where financial gain could arise, the culpability of the offender may be reduced where it can be shown that the offender did not seek to gain financially from the conduct and did not in fact do so.

Effective compliance and ethics programme

Self-reporting, co-operation and acceptance of responsibility

Where an offender has self-reported to the authorities, particularly in circumstances where the offence may otherwise have gone undetected, this should reduce the sentence.

Good character and/or exemplary conduct

This factor may apply whether or not the offender has previous convictions. Evidence that an offender has demonstrated positive good character through, for example, charitable works may reduce the sentence.

Steps 5 to 7

The court should now 'step back' and, using the factors set out in steps five, six and seven, review whether the sentence as a whole meets, in a fair way, the objectives of punishment, deterrence and removal of gain derived through the commission of the offence. At steps five to seven, the court may increase or reduce the proposed fine reached at step four, if necessary moving outside the range.

Step 5 – Ensure that the combination of financial orders (compensation, confiscation if appropriate, and fine) removes any economic benefit derived from the offending

The court should remove any economic benefit the offender has derived through the commission of the offence including avoided costs, operating savings and any gain made as a direct result of the offence.

In some water pollution cases there may be little obvious gain. However, there may still be some avoidance of cost which might have caused or contributed to the breach. Any costs avoided will be considered as economic benefit.

Where it is not possible to calculate or estimate the economic benefit, the court may wish to draw on information from the enforcing authorities about the general costs of operating within the law.

Step 6 – Check whether the proposed fine based on turnover is proportionate to the means of the offender

The combination of financial orders must be sufficiently substantial to have a real economic impact which will bring home to both management and shareholders the need to improve regulatory compliance. Whether the fine will have the effect of putting the offender out of business will be relevant; in some bad cases this may be an acceptable consequence.

In considering the ability of the offending organisation to pay any financial penalty, the court can take into account the power to allow time for payment or to order that the amount be paid in instalments.

Step 7 – Consider other factors that may warrant adjustment of the proposed fine

The court should consider any further factors that are relevant to ensuring that the proposed fine is proportionate having regard to the means of the offender and the seriousness of the offence.

Where the fine will fall on public or charitable bodies, the fine should normally be substantially reduced if the offending organisation is able to demonstrate the proposed fine would have a significant impact on the provision of their services.

The non-exhaustive list below contains additional factual elements the court should consider in deciding whether an increase or reduction to the proposed fine is required:

- Whether the fine impairs offender's ability to make restitution to victims;
- The impact of the fine on offender's ability to improve conditions in the organisation to comply with the law;
- The impact of the fine on employment of staff, service users, customers and local economy.

When sentencing organisations the fine must be sufficiently substantial to have a real economic impact which will bring home to both management and shareholders the need to comply with the law. The court should ensure that the effect of the fine (particularly if it will result in closure of the business) is proportionate to the gravity of the offence.

Step 8 – Consider any factors which indicate a reduction, such as assistance to the prosecution

The court should take into account sections 73 and 74 of the Serious Organised Crime and Police Act 2005 (assistance by defendants: reduction or review of sentence) and any other rule of law by virtue of which an offender may receive a discounted sentence in consequence of assistance given (or offered) to the prosecutor or investigator.

Step 9 – Reduction for guilty pleas

The court should take account of any potential reduction for a guilty plea in accordance with section 144 of the Criminal Justice Act 2003 and the guideline for Reduction in Sentence for a Guilty Plea (where first hearing is on or after 1 June 2017, or first hearing before 1 June 2017).

Step 10 – Ancillary orders

In all cases, the court must consider whether to make ancillary orders. These may include:

Forfeiture of vehicle

The court may order the forfeiture of a vehicle used in or for the purposes of the commission of the offence in accordance with section 33C of the Environmental Protection Act 1990.

Deprivation of property

Where section 33C of the Environmental Protection Act 1990 does not apply, the court may order the offender be deprived of property used to commit crime or intended for that purpose in accordance with section 143 of the Powers of Criminal Courts (Sentencing) Act 2000. In considering whether to make an order under section 143, the court must have regard to the value of the property and the likely effects on the offender of making the order taken together with any other order the court makes.

Remediation

Where an offender is convicted of an offence under regulation 38(1), (2) or (3) of the Environmental Permitting (England and Wales) Regulations 2010, a court may order the offender to take steps to remedy the cause of the offence within a specified period in accordance with regulation 44 of the Environmental Permitting (England and Wales) Regulations 2010.

Step 11 – Totality principle

If sentencing an offender for more than one offence, or where the offender is already serving a sentence, consider whether the total sentence is just and proportionate to the offending behaviour.

Step 12 – Reasons

Section 174 of the Criminal Justice Act 2003 imposes a duty to give reasons for, and explain the effect of, the sentence.

Other environmental offences

In sentencing other relevant and analogous environmental offences, the court should refer to the sentencing approach in steps one to three and five to seven of the guideline, adjusting the starting points and ranges bearing in mind the statutory maxima for those offences.

Remediation

It is open to the Courts to impose a remediation order following a conviction for an offence contrary to Regulation 38(1), (2) or (3) of EPR 2016 in addition to or instead of a punishment pursuant to Regulation 39. The power to make a remediation order is found in Regulation 44 EPR 2016.

Reg 44 Environmental Permitting (England and Wales) Regulations 2016

> **44.— Power of court to order cause of offence to be remedied**
>
> (1) This regulation applies where a person is convicted of an offence under regulation 38(1), (2) or (3) in respect of a matter which appears to the court to be a matter which it is in the person's power to remedy.
>
> (2) In addition to or instead of a punishment imposed under regulation 39, the court may order the person to take such steps for remedying the matter within such period as may be specified in the order.
>
> (3) The period may be extended, or further extended, by order of the court on an application made before the end of the period or the extended period, as the case may be.

(4) If a person is ordered to remedy a matter, that person is not liable under regulation 38 in respect of that matter during the period or the extended period.

In force: 1 January 2017

General observations

A remediation order is dependent on the Court assessing that the matter is one that is within the "person's power to remedy". To this extent, it must be means-tested.

A remediation order may be made "in addition to or instead of" a separate penalty for the offence.

No penalty is specified for breach of a remediation order. However, a failure to comply with a remediation order will amount to a contempt of court and/or will be considered as an aggravating feature in any subsequent criminal proceedings.

R (on the application of the Environment Agency) v Tapecrown Ltd[55]:

> "23. It seems to us that the order under CPR 70.2A did not constitute an order of the court in the exercise of its jurisdiction to punish for contempt of court. The court had already exercised that jurisdiction and was making an order consequent on the failure of Tapecrown to comply with the remediation order made in September 2015.
>
> 24. This analysis is supported by the terms of" CPR 70.2A itself:
>
> "70.2A Court may order act to be done at expense of disobedient party

[55] [2019] 1 W.L.R. 3394; [2019] Env. L.R. 3

(1) In this rule 'disobedient party' means a party who has not complied with a mandatory order, an injunction or a judgment or order for the specific performance of a contract.

(2) Subject to paragraph (4), if a *mandatory order, an injunction or a judgment or order for the specific performance of a contract is not complied with, the court may direct that the act required to be done may, so far as practicable, be done by another person, being—*

(a) the party by whom the order or judgment was obtained; or

(b) *some other person appointed by the court.*

(3) Where paragraph (2) applies—

(a) *the costs to another person of doing the act will be borne by the disobedient party*

(b) *upon the act being done the expenses incurred may be ascertained in such manner as the court directs;* and

(c) *execution may issue against the disobedient party* for the amount so ascertained and for costs.

(4) Paragraph (2) is *without prejudice to* —

(a) the court's powers under section 39 of the Senior Courts Act 1981; and

(b) *the court's powers to punish the disobedient party for contempt.*" (our italics)

25. The italicised words, and in particular those at paragraph 4, emphasise that what the court is doing is securing compliance with the previously made remediation order and that this is a process independent of the court's power to punish for contempt of court. The foundation for the CPR 70.2A order is not

the contempt proceedings but the remediation order, made long before there was any question of contempt of court."

Sentencing Individuals

The Guideline for Individuals largely mirrors the steps identified for sentencing organisations, although the penalties that can be imposed are quite different.

Starting points and ranges

Deliberate

Offence category	**Starting Point**	**Range**
Deliberate		
Category 1	18 months' custody	1 – 3 years' custody
Category 2	1 year's custody	26 weeks' – 18 months' custody
Category 3	Band F fine	Band E fine or medium level community order – 26 weeks' custody
Category 4	Band E fine	Band D fine or low-level community order– Band E fine

Reckless

Offence category	Starting Point	Range
Reckless		
Category 1	26 weeks' custody	Band F fine or high-level community order – 12 months' custody
Category 2	Band F fine	Band E fine or medium level community order – 26 weeks' custody
Category 3	Band E fine	Band D fine or low-level community order – Band E fine
Category 4	Band D fine	Band C fine – Band D fine

Negligent

Offence category	Starting Point	Range
Negligent		
Category 1	Band F fine	Band E fine or medium level community order – 26 weeks' custody
Category 2	Band E fine	Band D fine or low-level community order – Band E fine
Category 3	Band D fine	Band C fine – Band D fine
Category 4	Band C fine	Band B fine – Band C fine

Low / No culpability

Offence category	Starting Point	Range
Low / No culpability		
Category 1	Band D fine	Band C fine – Band D fine
Category 2	Band C fine	Band B fine – Band C fine
Category 3	Band B fine	Band A fine – Band B fine
Category 4	Band A fine	Conditional discharge – Band A fine

Fines

	Starting point	Range
Fine Band A	50% of relevant weekly income	25 – 75% of relevant weekly income
Fine Band B	100% of relevant weekly income	75 – 125% of relevant weekly income
Fine Band C	150% of relevant weekly income	125 – 175% of relevant weekly income
Fine Band D	250% of relevant weekly income	200 – 300% of relevant weekly income
Fine Band E	400% of relevant weekly income	300 – 500% of relevant weekly income
Fine Band F	600% of relevant weekly income	00 – 700% of relevant weekly income

The court should determine the appropriate level of fine in accordance with this guideline and section 164 of the Criminal Justice Act 2003, which requires that the fine must reflect the seriousness of the offence and that the court must take into account the financial circumstances of the offender.

Where possible, if a financial penalty is imposed, it should remove any economic benefit the offender has derived through the commission of the offence including avoided costs, operating savings and any gain made as a direct result of the offence.

The fine should meet, in a fair and proportionate way, the objectives of punishment, deterrence and the removal of gain derived through the commission of the offence; it should not be cheaper to offend than to comply with the law.

In considering economic benefit, the court should avoid double recovery. Where the means of the offender are limited, priority should be given to compensation (where applicable) over payment of any other financial penalty.

Where it is not possible to calculate or estimate the economic benefit, the court may wish to draw on information from the enforcing authorities about the general costs of operating within the law.

Obtaining financial information:

It is for the offender to disclose to the court such data relevant to their financial position as will enable it to assess what they can reasonably afford to pay. If necessary, the court may compel the disclosure of an individual offender's financial circumstances pursuant to section 162 of the Criminal Justice Act 2003. In the absence of such disclosure, or where the court is not satisfied that it has been given sufficient reliable information, the court will be entitled to draw reasonable inferences as to the offender's means from evidence it has heard and from all the circumstances of the case. In setting a fine, the court may conclude that the offender is able to pay any fine imposed unless the offender has supplied financial information to the contrary.

Community orders

The seriousness of the offence should be the initial factor in determining which requirements to include in a community order. Offence specific guidelines refer to three sentencing levels within the community order band based on offence seriousness (low, medium and high). The culpability and harm present in the offence(s) should be considered to identify which of the three sentencing levels within the community order band is appropriate.

Low	Medium	High
Offences only just cross community order threshold, where the seriousness of the offence or the nature of the offender's record means that a discharge or fine is inappropriate In general, only one requirement will be appropriate and the length may be curtailed if additional requirements are necessary	Offences that obviously fall within the community order band	Offences only just fall below the custody threshold or the custody threshold is crossed but a community order is more appropriate in the circumstances More intensive sentences which combine two or more requirements may be appropriate

Suitable requirements might include: Any appropriate rehabilitative requirement(s) 40 – 80 hours of unpaid work Curfew requirement for example up to 16 hours per day for a few weeks Exclusion requirement, for a few months Prohibited activity requirement Attendance centre requirement (where available)	Suitable requirements might include: Any appropriate rehabilitative requirement(s) 80 – 150 hours of unpaid work Curfew requirement for example up to 16 hours for 2 – 3 months Exclusion requirement lasting in the region of 6 months Prohibited activity requirement	Suitable requirements might include: Any appropriate rehabilitative requirement(s) 150 – 300 hours of unpaid work Curfew requirement for example up to 16 hours per day for 4 – 12 months Exclusion requirement lasting in the region of 12 months

* If order does not contain a punitive requirement, suggested fine levels are indicated below:

BAND A FINE	**BAND B FINE**	**BAND C FINE**

Custodial sentences

The approach to the imposition of a custodial sentence should be as follows:

1) Has the custody threshold been passed?

A custodial sentence must not be imposed unless the offence or the combination of the offence and one or more offences associated with it was so serious that neither a fine alone nor a community sentence can be justified for the offence.

However, a custodial sentence might not be appropriate where a community order could provide sufficient punishment and rehabilitation or where the custodial sentence can be suspended.

The imposition of a custodial sentence is both punishment and a deterrent. To ensure that the overall terms of the suspended sentence are commensurate with offence seriousness, care must be taken to ensure requirements imposed are not excessive. A court wishing to impose onerous or intensive requirements should reconsider whether a community sentence might be more appropriate.

Mitigating factors particular to sentencing individuals

Many of the mitigating factors identified in the Guideline are identical for both organisations and individuals. The factors set out below are only those relevant to individuals.

Mental disorder or learning disability, where linked to the commission of the offence

Serious medical conditions requiring urgent, intensive or long-term treatment

Age and/or lack of maturity where it affects the responsibility of the offender

Age and/or lack of maturity can affect: the offender's responsibility for the offence and the effect of the sentence on the offender.

Sole or primary carer for dependent relatives

Fines in the magistrates' court

All environmental offences are subject to a fine. Many of the more serious environmental offences are also subject to a custodial sentence.

Standard scale. Summary offences sometimes refer to the level of the fine by reference to level 1-5 on the "standard scale" (*section 37(2), Criminal Justice Act 1982*). These are currently set at:

- Level 1: £200.
- Level 2: £500.
- Level 3: £1,000.
- Level 4: £2,500.
- Unlimited fine.

Fines in the Crown Court

Environmental offences are subject to an unlimited fine in the Crown Court.

R v Thames Water Utilities Limited [2019] EWCA Crim 1344

A fine of £2 million imposed on a water company after it pleaded guilty to an environmental offence by recklessly causing a discharge of untreated sewage into a brook was neither wrong in principle nor manifestly excessive.

In *R v McIntosh* [2019] EWCA Crim 231 it was held that a sentencing judge had been entitled to impose a community order with unpaid work requirement, a five-year director disqualification, and a prosecution costs order on a former waste management company director who had pleaded guilty to environmental offences. The director had been negligent, and the company had repeatedly ignored regulations and compliance requirements.

The prosecution's costs

The court will usually decide at the sentencing hearing how much of the prosecution's costs the defendant will have to pay. Investigative costs, as well as legal costs, can be claimed. In environmental prosecutions, these can exceed the fine. In *R v Associated Octel Company Ltd [1996] EWCA Crim 1237*, the Court of Appeal upheld a fine of £150,000 and the regulator's legal and investigative costs of £142,000. Although that case related to a health and safety offence, it is likely that the same approach would be followed by a court when sentencing an environmental offence.

Costs, Reputation and Orders

- **Payment of fines and costs.** The court will set a time limit by which a fine and the prosecution's costs must be paid.

- **Publicity.** A conviction for an environmental offence may lead to adverse publicity as the EA publicises environmental convictions, including sentences, on its website.

- **Enforcement of orders and injunctions.** The prosecuting authority may obtain an injunction if the offenders fail to undertake any remedial work.

CHAPTER ELEVEN
CONFISCATION

Confiscation order

The Crown Court has the power to make a confiscation order, section 6 *Proceeds of Crime Act 2002* (POCA)). The crown court must proceed to a confiscation hearing where either a defendant has been convicted of an offence before the crown court or committed by a magistrates' court for sentence at the crown court and either the prosecutor asks the court to proceed to a confiscation hearing, or the court believes it is appropriate to do so. A magistrates' court does not have such a power but if the prosecutor asks it to send the case to the crown court to consider a confiscation order, it must do so, section 70 POCA. The crown court retains a discretion to refuse to make a confiscation order where the victim has initiated civil proceedings or where making a confiscation order would constitute an abuse of process.

A confiscation order requires the offender to pay an amount that reflects the financial benefit they have gained from the offence. Where there can only be a financial penalty, the confiscation proceedings must precede the sentence so as to avoid double accounting, section 13(2) POCA.

The courts have confirmed that the aims of confiscation are, to punish convicted offenders, deterrence, and to reduce profits for funding future crimes, *R v Rezvi* [2002] UKHL 1.

The POCA 2002 regime applies to offences committed after 24 March 2003.

The court first has to decide whether the defendant has a criminal lifestyle. The court will conclude that a defendant has a criminal lifestyle if he satisfies one of the following criteria:

- The defendant has been convicted of an offence specified in Schedule 2 to POCA 2002.

- The conduct forms part of a course of criminal activity.

- The offence was committed over a period of at least six months, and the defendant has obtained a benefit from the conduct of at least £5,000.

Where the court finds that the defendant has a criminal lifestyle, it must decide whether he has benefited from his general criminal conduct.
If the court decides that the defendant has benefited from general criminal conduct then the following assumptions apply:

- Any property transferred to the defendant within the period of six years ending on the day on which proceedings were started was obtained by him as a result of his general criminal conduct.

- Any property held by him at any time after the date of conviction was obtained by him as a result of his general criminal conduct.

- Any expenditure incurred by him within a period of six years ending with the date on which the proceedings were started against him was met from property obtained by him as a result of his general criminal conduct.

- Any property obtained or assumed to have been obtained by the defendant is free of any other interest in the property.

  (Section 10 *POCA 2002.*)

These assumptions apply unless they are demonstrated by the defendant to be incorrect (to a civil standard), or where to apply them would cause a serious risk of injustice.

If the court decides that the defendant does not have a criminal lifestyle then it must decide whether he has benefited from his particular criminal conduct. It should then ask itself, how much he has benefitted from that particular criminal conduct and what the recoverable amount is.

Benefit from Criminal Conduct

A defendant benefits from criminal conduct if he "obtains" property and property is obtained by a person if he obtains an interest in it, section 84(2)(b). The burden of proof lies on the prosecution to the civil standard (but see *Briggs-Price* [2009] UKHL 19). In *May* [2008] UKHL 28 the court held that "obtains" connotes "a power of disposition or control". A defendant cannot and should not be deprived of what he never obtained or its equivalent, *Jennings v CPS* [2008] UKHL 29. To count as benefit the property must have been obtained as a result of or in connection with the criminal conduct

In *R v Ryder; R v Green* [2020] EWCA Crim 1110 the Court of Appeal held, that a Recorder, when making a confiscation order against the owners of a waste management site following their conviction for operating a regulated facility without an environmental permit, contrary to the Environmental Permitting (England and Wales) Regulations 2010 Pt 2 (1) reg.12(1)(a) and reg.38(1)(a), had not erred in including in the figure for benefit from criminal conduct an asserted pecuniary advantage from the owners' avoidance of paying the costs of removal of waste from the site. The recorder had, however, erred when determining the available amount in including one owner's share in a jointly-owned property without determining the validity of an asserted equitable charge over the property.

In *R v Rory J Holbrook Limited* [2015] EWCA Crim 1908, the court upheld a £30,000 fine and a confiscation order that included the income, not just the profit, accrued by a company that had pleaded guilty to depositing and disposing of waste without the relevant environmental and waste management permits. R had contended that the judge erred in applying the distinction made in *R. v King (Scott) [2014] EWCA Crim 621, [2014] 2 Cr. App. R. (S.) 54, [2014] 4 WLUK 120* between lawful activities tainted by illegality and an entirely illegal undertaking, and that its own conduct had not been generally unlawful. Those contentions misunderstood *King*. The whole of R's activity at the golf course site was unlawful due to absence of the relevant permits, *King* applied. In those circumstances it was not a disproportionate result to remove from the unlawful business the proceeds it had generated. The judge had calculated the benefit obtained as a result of the offences, and assessed whether her approach was disproportionate so as to be incompatible with ECHR Protocol 1 art.1. That approach was justified. R had bypassed the regulatory regime for 12 months, engendered the risk of environmental harm, and impacted on the activities of legitimate operators while enhancing its own position. To find a recoverable benefit on the basis solely of profit was not appropriate (paras 18-19).

In *R v Morrow* [2020] Env. L.R. 21 a judge had erred in determining for the purpose of confiscation proceedings an issue as to whether material was "waste" on the basis of submissions when significant issues of fact were disputed or unknown, effectively precluding relevant evidence being adduced by the defendant. The court observed that parties should agree a factual basis of plea and attempt to resolve confiscation order applications by agreement to avoid the need for time-consuming and costly hearings.

Benefit does not mean profit, *May* [2008] UKHL 28. No discount can be given to reflect income which the defendant would have derived from the loser had there been no misconduct, *Richards* [2005] EWCA Crim 491.

R v Christopher Morgan[56]

> "On the assumption that the judge was correct to conclude that the defendant had engaged in a disposal operation, he was also correct to conclude that he had, by engaging in unlawful unlicensed activity, thereby obtained a pecuniary advantage in the sum of £156,500. This is because the defendant had evaded landfill tax and licence fees and had avoided paying for other costs that he would have had to pay if the operation had been conducted lawfully"

[56] [2014] 1 WLR 3450

Recoverable Amount

Section 7 of POCA deals with this concept. The recoverable amount is an amount equal to the defendant's benefit from the conduct concerned. However if the defendant shows that the available amount is less than the benefit the recoverable amount is the value of the available amount or a nominal amount.

Proportionality

Any confiscation order must be is proportionate, *R v Waya [2012] UKSC 51*. In R v Morgan [2013] EWCA Crim 1307 the court held that a confiscation order in the sum of £156,500 which had been imposed on the appellant, who had pleaded guilty to offences concerning the unlawful deposit of waste material at an unlicensed landfill site, was not disproportionate so as to amount to a breach of the appellant's rights under the European Convention on Human Rights 1950 Protocol 1 art.1; further, the judge had been correct to assess the "benefit" obtained by the appellant by reference to the landfill tax, licence fees and other costs that he would have had to pay had the operation been conducted lawfully.

Imprisonment in Default

Where a confiscation order is made but is not paid, the defendant will serve a period of imprisonment in default. This does not apply to a company defendant. This default sentence is fixed by the court when the order is made. The defendant will still owe the confiscation sum, even when the default sentence is served. When paid this sum may be divided between HM Treasury and the investigators, prosecuting authority and HM Courts and Tribunals Service. A prosecution brought merely to facilitate this acquisition by a regulator or enforcement agency is likely to be unlawful.

Time to pay and period in default

Confiscation orders become payable on the day that they are made and the Court can only grant an extension if satisfied that the defendant is unable to comply. That discretion will be limited to situations where assets need to be realised and then only for 3 months (*section 11(3) POCA*). A subsequent application can be made, and if the court is satisfied that despite all reasonable efforts the defendant is unable to pay the amount within that period, then as long as the application is made before the expiry of that period, the court can extend the period in respect of the outstanding amount. This extension can only be up to six months.

Piercing the Corporate Veil

In law, a company is normally treated as having a separate legal person to that of its owners or shareholders. That legal entity is solely responsible for the debts it incurs and the credit it is entitled to. Lifting, or piercing, the corporate veil is a legal concept that enables the rights and the duties of a corporation to be treated as those of its shareholders, or more particularly in respect of confiscation proceedings, as the assets of the company.

In confiscation proceedings under the *Proceeds of Crime Act 2002*, monies received by a company can, depending on the particular facts of the case, be regarded as having been obtained by an individual when that individual was in a managing or directorial position within the company. Consequently, those monies may become an element in the individual's benefit obtained from criminal conduct, and subsequently subject to confiscation.

In *R v Seager [2009] EWCA Crim 1303* the judge also identified three situations when the corporate veil can be pierced: If an offender attempts to shelter behind a corporate façade, or veil to hide his crime and his benefits from it; where an offender acts in the name of a company leading to his conviction; and, where the transaction or business structures constitute a "device", "cloak" or "sham".

In *Jennings v CPS [2008] UKHL 29*, the court held there was no need to pierce the corporate veil given the meaning given to "benefit". The court stated the essence of what was meant by benefit was given by the verb "obtain", and whether in any given case a person had obtained any particular property was a question of fact. It did not mean "retain" or "keep" but contemplated that the defendant in question should have been instrumental in getting the property out of the crime. There was no separate requirement that the defendant must be shown to have "control" over the property.

The corporate veil is not pierced in any case where there is no evidence of dishonesty or impropriety, therefore, the profits made by a company from an inadvertent breach of a regulation by an individual cannot be confiscated from that individual, *R v Boyle Transport (Northern Ireland) Ltd [2016] EWCA Crim 19.* This position was supported by *R v Powell [2016] EWCA Crim 1043*, where the Court of Appeal refused the Crown's application for the costs of clearing up illegally disposed waste on the basis that such an approach would risk making every company director liable to the confiscation regime whenever a company broke the criminal law.

CHAPTER TWELVE
CIVIL SANCTIONS

Enforcement Undertakings

The Environment Agency may accept an Enforcement Undertaking from a person in a case where the Environment Agency has reasonable grounds to suspect that the person has committed an offence contract to Regulation 38(1), (2), (4), (5) or (6) of the Environmental Permitting (England and Wales) Regulations 2016.

Sch 26 Para 2 Environmental Permitting (England and Wales) Regulations 2016

2.— Contents of an enforcement undertaking

(1) An enforcement undertaking must specify—

(a) action to secure that the offence does not continue or recur,

(b) action to secure that the position is, so far as possible, restored to what it would have been if the offence had not been committed,

(c) action (including the payment of a sum of money) to benefit any person affected by the offence, or

(d) where restoration of the harm arising from the offence is not possible, action that will secure equivalent benefit or improvement to the environment.

(2) It must specify the period within which the action must be completed.

(3) It must include—

(a) a statement that the undertaking is given in accordance with this Schedule;

(b) the terms of the undertaking;

(c) how and when a person is considered to have discharged the undertaking.

(4) The enforcement undertaking may be varied, or the period within which the action must be completed may be extended, if both parties agree in writing.

Enforcement Undertakings can be an extremely effective and useful method of resolving issues relating to breaches of environmental legislation. They provide an opportunity for providing an appropriate environmental outcome to a case, as well as allowing for timely resolution of disputes. In a context where many of the offences relating to breaches of environmental legislation are strict liability, consideration of an Enforcement Undertaking is likely to be an attractive option.

However, despite the apparent benefits of Enforcement Undertakings, it is still not an option currently available to Natural Resources Wales, who remain constrained by current legislation as to the types of offences for which they can accept an Enforcement Undertaking. At the time of writing, for example, it is not open to NRW to accept an Enforcement Undertaking for a breach of the Environmental Permitting Regulations.

The approach of the Environment Agency in practice

Enforcement Undertakings are not a negotiation. They are intended to be a voluntary offer. Enforcement Undertakings can be either proactive or reactive. Often, given the strict liability nature of environmental offences, useful consideration can be given to an Enforcement Undertaking at an early stage in any investigation, particularly if the particular incident that is the subject of the investigation has not resulted in significant environmental harm.

Published guidance by the Environment Agency states that an Enforcement Undertaking will not normally be accepted for an incident or breach that has been classified under either CCS or CICS as a Category 1, unless there is, at most, low culpability or a Category 2, unless there is, at most, negligence.

However, much depends on the individual circumstances in any one case. The guidance also states that the Environment Agency will not normally accept an offer where legal proceedings have already been started, but it is not unknown to resolve ongoing cases by way of an Enforcement Undertaking even where criminal proceedings have reached the Crown Court.

The pro forma provided by the Environment Agency contains important guidance on what factors are considered as important in the consideration of an Enforcement Undertaking. In the experience of the authors, the following factors are significant and Enforcement Undertaking offers would be well advised to ensure that these are addressed:

- Being proactive so far as possible;
- Acting in good faith;
- Accepting liability;
- Demonstrating willingness with the Environment Agency;
- Promoting good corporate history;
- Ensuring that the specifics of Schedule 26 are met;
- Demonstrating high level/Board engagement with the incident and its causes.

The latter factor on Board level engagement is particularly important.

Most of the time it pays to have a good level of engagement with the Environment Agency prior to the making of any Enforcement Undertaking offer and to be pragmatic.

All accepted Enforcement Undertakings are publicised on the gov.uk website. The total cost of any actions does not equate to the figure published by the EA, which appears to be limited to the charitable contribution. There is also a brief summary of actions offered.

Challenging a refusal of an Enforcement Undertaking

Environment Agency guidance states:

> *"In light of the benefits of offering an Enforcement Undertaking, we expect the total cost of any actions (e.g. payments, restoration works, donations etc.) to go beyond the simple estimated financial gain or advantage, and equate to what might be expected if the case had been prosecuted."*

This approach, in light of the specific factors set out in Schedule 26, is not necessarily lawful but, at the time of publication, has never been challenged. It is highly unlikely that the Environment Agency would state, in reasons given justifying its refusal, that the value of the offer was not commensurate with the Sentencing Guideline.

However, there is high level of opacity in the Enforcement Undertaking process. The Panel that considers the offer will also consider representations made by either the officer in the case or the reviewing lawyer which the legal person making the offer will not have the opportunity to see, comment on or correct. There is no opportunity, save for perhaps within a covering letter accompanying the Enforcement Undertaking offer, the opportunity to address the Panel and it is quite likely that the legal person making the offer will not have access to the same information that the Panel has. There is, therefore, scope for a judicial review of the procedural fairness of the Enforcement Undertaking system in the event of an unfair refusal.

In practice, in the event that the value of the offer was simply too low, it is likely that this fact will be communicated in some way to the offeror, leaving open the opportunity to resubmit a higher offer.

Variable Monetary Penalties

The Environment Agency has the power, pursuant to the Regulatory Enforcement and Sanctions Act 2008, to impose a variable monetary penalty ('VMP') of an offender up to a value of £250,000. Published guidance indicates that the Environment Agency use a similar stepped approach to the Sentencing Guideline in order to calculate the level of VMP. This requires an assessment of culpability and harm, consideration of the size of the organisation or financial circumstances of the individual and further steps such as removing the economic benefit and proportionality.

The published guidance is arguably flawed. It states that, as the maximum penalty under a VMP is £250,000, then the Environment Agency will reduce the starting point set out in the Environmental Guideline by a factor of 4 to reflect the statutory maximum in determining the appropriate starting point for a VMP. However, this fails to take account of the fact that there is no upper maximum limit on a financial penalty that can be imposed by a Crown Court. Furthermore, the highest quoted figure in the Guideline for a deliberate category 1 offence is £3 million, at the very top of the range. The starting point for this offence is in fact one third of the quoted maximum figure in the range. As a result, it could be argued that if the Environment Agency was applying a VMP penalty system proportionate to the Definitive Guideline, the starting point for a deliberate category 1 offence should in fact be one third of £250,000, namely £83,333. Adopting a starting point that is in fact the maximum penalty that could be imposed under a VMP does not allow room to move upwards in the event of aggravating features or previous convictions and arguably sets the starting point at too high a level for each individual offence. In addition, no credit is given for resolving a case by way of a VMP.

Appeals

Those who are made the subject of a VMP may appeal to a tribunal within the General Regulatory Chamber. The grounds of appeal against the imposition of a civil sanction will be one of the following:

- decision was based on an error of fact
- decision was wrong in law
- decision was unreasonable
- amount is unreasonable
- any other reason

There is therefore a wide scope for grounds of appeal. In practice, as VMPs are so infrequently used by the Environment Agency, no appeal has ever been heard.

MORE BOOKS BY LAW BRIEF PUBLISHING

A selection of our other titles available now:-

'Covid-19, Homeworking and the Law – The Essential Guide to Employment and GDPR Issues' by Forbes Solicitors
'Covid-19, Force Majeure and Frustration of Contracts – The Essential Guide' by Keith Markham
'Covid-19 and Criminal Law – The Essential Guide' by Ramya Nagesh
'Covid-19 and Family Law in England and Wales – The Essential Guide' by Safda Mahmood
'Covid-19 and the Implications for Planning Law – The Essential Guide' by Bob Mc Geady & Meyric Lewis
'Covid-19, Residential Property, Equity Release and Enfranchisement – The Essential Guide' by Paul Sams and Louise Uphill
'Covid-19, Brexit and the Law of Commercial Leases – The Essential Guide' by Mark Shelton
'Covid-19 and the Law Relating to Food in the UK and Republic of Ireland – The Essential Guide' by Ian Thomas
'A Practical Guide to the General Data Protection Regulation (GDPR) – 2nd Edition' by Keith Markham
'Ellis on Credit Hire – Sixth Edition' by Aidan Ellis & Tim Kevan
'A Practical Guide to Working with Litigants in Person and McKenzie Friends in Family Cases' by Stuart Barlow
'Protecting Unregistered Brands: A Practical Guide to the Law of Passing Off' by Lorna Brazell
'A Practical Guide to Secondary Liability and Joint Enterprise Post-Jogee' by Joanne Cecil & James Mehigan

'A Practical Guide to the Pre-Action RTA Claims Protocol for Personal Injury Lawyers' by Antonia Ford
'A Practical Guide to Neighbour Disputes and the Law' by Alexander Walsh
'A Practical Guide to Forfeiture of Leases' by Mark Shelton
'A Practical Guide to Coercive Control for Legal Practitioners and Victims' by Rachel Horman
'A Practical Guide to Rights Over Airspace and Subsoil' by Daniel Gatty
'Tackling Disclosure in the Criminal Courts – A Practitioner's Guide' by Narita Bahra QC & Don Ramble
'A Practical Guide to the Law of Driverless Cars – Second Edition' by Alex Glassbrook, Emma Northey & Scarlett Milligan
'A Practical Guide to TOLATA Claims' by Greg Williams
'Artificial Intelligence – The Practical Legal Issues' by John Buyers
'A Practical Guide to the Law of Prescription in Scotland' by Andrew Foyle
'A Practical Guide to the Construction and Rectification of Wills and Trust Instruments' by Edward Hewitt
'A Practical Guide to the Law of Bullying and Harassment in the Workplace' by Philip Hyland
'How to Be a Freelance Solicitor: A Practical Guide to the SRA-Regulated Freelance Solicitor Model' by Paul Bennett
'A Practical Guide to Prison Injury Claims' by Malcolm Johnson
'A Practical Guide to the Small Claims Track' by Dominic Bright
'A Practical Guide to Advising Clients at the Police Station' by Colin Stephen McKeown-Beaumont
'A Practical Guide to Antisocial Behaviour Injunctions' by Iain Wightwick
'Practical Mediation: A Guide for Mediators, Advocates, Advisers, Lawyers, and Students in Civil, Commercial, Business, Property, Workplace, and Employment Cases' by Jonathan Dingle with John Sephton
'The Mini-Pupillage Workbook' by David Boyle

'A Practical Guide to Crofting Law' by Brian Inkster

'A Practical Guide to Spousal Maintenance' by Liz Cowell

'A Practical Guide to the Law of Domain Names and Cybersquatting' by Andrew Clemson

'A Practical Guide to the Law of Gender Pay Gap Reporting' by Harini Iyengar

'A Practical Guide to the Rights of Grandparents in Children Proceedings' by Stuart Barlow

'NHS Whistleblowing and the Law' by Joseph England

'Employment Law and the Gig Economy' by Nigel Mackay & Annie Powell

'A Practical Guide to Noise Induced Hearing Loss (NIHL) Claims' by Andrew Mckie, Ian Skeate, Gareth McAloon

'An Introduction to Beauty Negligence Claims – A Practical Guide for the Personal Injury Practitioner' by Greg Almond

'Intercompany Agreements for Transfer Pricing Compliance' by Paul Sutton

'Zen and the Art of Mediation' by Martin Plowman

'A Practical Guide to the SRA Principles, Individual and Law Firm Codes of Conduct 2019 – What Every Law Firm Needs to Know' by Paul Bennett

'A Practical Guide to Adoption for Family Lawyers' by Graham Pegg

'A Practical Guide to Industrial Disease Claims' by Andrew Mckie & Ian Skeate

'A Practical Guide to Redundancy' by Philip Hyland

'A Practical Guide to Vicarious Liability' by Mariel Irvine

'A Practical Guide to Applications for Landlord's Consent and Variation of Leases' by Mark Shelton

'A Practical Guide to Relief from Sanctions Post-Mitchell and Denton' by Peter Causton

'A Practical Guide to Equity Release for Advisors' by Paul Sams

'A Practical Guide to Unlawful Eviction and Harassment' by Stephanie Lovegrove

'A Practical Guide to the Law Relating to Food' by Ian Thomas

'A Practical Guide to Financial Services Claims' by Chris Hegarty
'The Law of Houses in Multiple Occupation: A Practical Guide to HMO Proceedings' by Julian Hunt
'A Practical Guide to Unlawful Eviction and Harassment' by Stephanie Lovegrove
'A Practical Guide to Solicitor and Client Costs' by Robin Dunne
'Occupiers, Highways and Defective Premises Claims: A Practical Guide Post-Jackson – 2nd Edition' by Andrew Mckie
'A Practical Guide to Financial Ombudsman Service Claims' by Adam Temple & Robert Scrivenor
'A Practical Guide to Advising Schools on Employment Law' by Jonathan Holden
'A Practical Guide to Running Housing Disrepair and Cavity Wall Claims: 2nd Edition' by Andrew Mckie & Ian Skeate
'A Practical Guide to Holiday Sickness Claims – 2nd Edition' by Andrew Mckie & Ian Skeate
'Arguments and Tactics for Personal Injury and Clinical Negligence Claims' by Dorian Williams
'A Practical Guide to QOCS and Fundamental Dishonesty' by James Bentley
'A Practical Guide to Drone Law' by Rufus Ballaster, Andrew Firman, Eleanor Clot
'A Practical Guide to Compliance for Personal Injury Firms Working With Claims Management Companies' by Paul Bennett
'A Practical Guide to the Landlord and Tenant Act 1954: Commercial Tenancies' by Richard Hayes & David Sawtell
'A Practical Guide to Dog Law for Owners and Others' by Andrea Pitt
'RTA Allegations of Fraud in a Post-Jackson Era: The Handbook – 2nd Edition' by Andrew Mckie
'RTA Personal Injury Claims: A Practical Guide Post-Jackson' by Andrew Mckie
'On Experts: CPR35 for Lawyers and Experts' by David Boyle
'An Introduction to Personal Injury Law' by David Boyle

'A Practical Guide to Chronic Pain Claims' by Pankaj Madan
'A Practical Guide to Claims Arising from Fatal Accidents' by James Patience
'A Practical Guide to Subtle Brain Injury Claims' by Pankaj Madan

www.ingramcontent.com/pod-product-compliance
Lightning Source LLC
LaVergne TN
LVHW052326200926
848481LV00002B/678

* 9 7 8 1 9 1 2 6 8 7 0 9 1 *